Patterns of poverty across Europe

Richard Berthoud

INSTITUTE FOR SOCIAL
& ECONOMIC RESEARCH

First published in Great Britain in March 2004 by

The Policy Press
University of Bristol
Fourth Floor, Beacon House
Queen's Road
Bristol BS8 1QU
UK

Tel no +44 (0)117 331 4054
Fax no +44 (0)117 331 4093
E-mail tpp-info@bristol.ac.uk
www.policypress.org.uk

ISBN 1 86134 574 7

Richard Berthoud is a Research Professor at the Institute for Social and Economic Research, University of Essex, UK.

Cover design by Qube Design Associates, Bristol
Front cover: Photograph supplied by kind permission of Panos Pictures
Printed in Great Britain by Henry Ling Ltd, Dorchester

Contents

List of tables and figures

Tables

Figures

Acknowledgements

This report is part of a programme of research on *The dynamics of social change in Europe*, undertaken by the European Panel Analysis Group (EPAG), and supported by the European Commission under its Fifth Framework. For other outputs from the programme, see Berthoud and Iacovou (2004) and www.iser.essex.ac.uk/epag/pubs

The data from the European Community Household Panel survey (ECHP) were supplied by Eurostat.

I am very grateful to Tony Mathys of the UK Data Archive for drawing the maps in Chapters 5 and 6; to Karol Kuhl and Richard Layte for supplying additional statistics; and to Tony Atkinson, Dave Gordon, Stephen Jenkins and Tim Smeeding for valuable comments.

Of course, none of these organisations or individuals necessarily endorses the conclusions of the analysis, which are the author's responsibility.

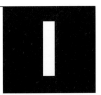

Geography, inequality and poverty: an EU perspective

Low income has been seen as a cross-European problem at least since the launch of the First Community Programme to Combat Poverty in 1975. It remains a key issue as EU institutions have increasingly focused on the development of social, as well as narrowly economic, policies. The Council meeting in Lisbon in March 2000 declared that 'steps must be taken to make a decisive impact on the eradication of poverty'.

If the Union is concerned to eradicate poverty, it is important to have a clear idea of where poor people live. In which European countries is poverty most common? What is it that links the countries with high poverty rates and distinguishes them from those where poverty is rare? Is 'country' really the best way of distinguishing between rich and poor areas? Perhaps the main variation is between high- and low-poverty regions within countries. If there are important variations between the 15 current member states, what will be the impact of expanding the Union over the next few years, introducing countries with much lower levels of aggregate income, and very different political trajectories, from those of the existing members? So the question of 'where are the poor?' is closely bound up with the question 'who are the poor, and how many of them are there?'.

This study reports on an analysis of the distribution of household income across the whole of the 15-country EU, breaking down the range of inequality by country, and by region within country. It illustrates substantial differences in the spatial distribution of poverty, depending on whether regional, national or Europe-wide benchmarks are used to define a 'relative' poverty line. And it tests two possible methods of calibrating poverty lines, to

contribute to an empirical approach to the choice of benchmark.

Eurostat publishes a standard league table showing the proportion of households in poverty in each member state, based on the now-standard definition of having an equivalised income below 60% of the national median: ranging from 9% in Denmark to 22% in Portugal (Eurostat, 2003). That provides the most immediate answer to the question addressed here. But by focusing exclusively on households' position in the distribution of income within their own member state, the standard counts provide only a restricted view of the geographical and political variations in the extent of poverty. Even if the standard definition (60% of national median) is retained, we need to ask where the poor are concentrated *within* each member state, and where they are concentrated *across* member states occupying different locations in the European space. It is also worth considering whether alternative definitions of 'low income' would provide different maps of the distribution of poverty across areas.

By borrowing the analytical assumptions from a whole range of income and poverty research traditions, the study raises a series of questions about the frame of reference for international comparisons, especially when the 'nations' being compared are members of a Union that has a perspective of its own. The analysis makes no attempt to test assumptions about the overall level of poverty in the Union; but it shows that alternative assumptions about the way income-poverty lines are defined cross-nationally have important implications for the geographical distribution of poverty. Since (in this context) 'geographical distribution' includes variations in the prevalence of poverty between EU member states, important issues both of policy and of political structure depend on the answer.

There is a huge literature on the distribution of household income, and the extent of income poverty, within any country (Atkinson and Bourguignon, 2000). Occasionally this extends to an analysis of variations in income levels, and in the prevalence of poverty, between regions within a country, or even smaller geographical units (for example, Jargowsky, 1996; Nolan with others, 1998; Berthoud, 2001). Where geographical comparisons are made within a country, the frame of reference is almost invariably the national distribution of income – regional averages are compared within the national framework, but the shape of the distribution of income within each region is rarely analysed. Poverty lines are rarely set in relation to a regional benchmark[1]. Subject to technical questions about area variations in the cost of living, the standard against which household income or consumption should be compared is conventionally the same in Northern Ireland as in London, and the same in Sicily as in Lombardy. Because of the common national benchmark, it follows that there is usually a relatively large number of poor households in the regions (within a country) with low average incomes.

When incomes are being compared *between* countries, there are two distinct research traditions. One, probably the most commonly used in international economic discourse, compares the overall average incomes of each of the countries under study. The data are derived from the aggregate national accounts, and expressed in terms of the total national income scaled against the size of the country – GDP per head is the most commonly used measure. It is statistics such as these that enable us to know that the OECD countries of western Europe, North America, Australasia and Japan are so much richer than the poor countries of Africa and Asia; that some countries are catching up and others lagging behind. Closer to home, it is the same aggregate statistics that record Luxembourg as the richest and Portugal the poorest countries in the EU, while the candidate countries are significantly poorer than most of the current

member states (Eurostat, 2003). Note the use, in this analysis, of the words 'rich' and 'poor' to describe whole countries' positions in the international distribution of living standards. Note also the inference, in global terms, that 'the poor' tend to be people who live in low-income countries.

The national accounts are compiled by estimating the total annual flows of each type of income (earnings, company profits and so on) and then adding the components together. They cannot be used to analyse the distribution of income between households *within* a country, because income is not attributed to households at any stage in the procedure. Comparisons between countries of their within-country inequalities require household survey data that have been compiled in a similar way in each country (Smeeding with others, 1990). It is only in recent years that the Luxembourg Income Study has assembled comparable data from a sufficient number of countries for such analysis to be possible[2]. Some studies have undertaken detailed comparisons between two or three countries (for example, Atkinson with others, 1998); others have taken a broader brush approach to the comparison of a much larger number of countries (Atkinson with others, 1995; Atkinson, 2003). In most of these cross-country comparisons, the focus is on variations between countries in their within-country income inequalities; the income variations between countries are less often taken into account (Gottschalk and Smeeding, 2000).

One reason for taking between-country variations in average income into account in an analysis of within-countries' income distributions is that the within-country distribution may vary systematically according to the overall position of the country in the international income ladder. Smeeding (2000), in an important exception to the generalisation in the preceding paragraph, showed that if household incomes in each of several countries were all expressed in terms of a common metric based on purchasing power, the combination of high national income and wide inequality in the United States (compared with other OECD nations) would mean that the consumption standards at the top of the American distribution were much higher than those at the top of other nations' distributions, but that the

---

[1] Exceptions are Rainwater with others (1999) and Jesuit with others (2003), who compare 'state' poverty lines within the US and other federal countries with 'regional' poverty lines in European countries.

[2] www.lisproject.org

consumption of households at the lower end of the American distribution was little different from that of their equivalents elsewhere. And, as will be seen later, both the width and the shape of the income distributions of EU member states are systematically related to the countries' overall average incomes.

This means that overall national incomes can provide an important analytical context for comparisons of national inequalities and relative poverty rates. Where researchers have selected a limited range of countries, often on the basis of the availability of data, it has not been possible to provide direct estimates of the relative importance of between-country and within-country variations. But if the countries analysed consist of all the members of some definable group of countries, it is possible to consider the group as a whole as having an average income and a distribution between households, and to partition that overall distribution into its components: between-countries and within-countries.

The European Union is not only a definable group of countries; it is in many senses a political entity. Data about household incomes in all 15 countries are now available in reasonably consistent form, and it is possible to look at the income of 'Europe' in a way that is not simply a pastiche of the incomes of each of several unconnected countries. This allows us to investigate the distribution of income across European countries in exactly the same way as one might study the distribution of income across British or Italian regions. Previous analyses of the distribution of income across 'Europe' (as variously defined) have assembled distributional statistics from more than one survey (Atkinson, 1995; Beblo and Knau, 2001); but the European Community Household Panel (ECHP) now allows analysis of incomes and poverty rates across the whole of the 15-country union, treated for some purposes as a single geographical or political entity.

It also, of course, allows us to investigate the distribution of income across European regions. By adopting an EU-wide perspective and calculating incomes on a common yardstick of purchasing power, it is possible to dissolve national boundaries in our mind's eye and plot the high points and low points of prosperity across the Union. Does it make sense to compare a small country like Denmark with Germany as a whole, or would the neighbouring German region of Schleswig-Holstein provide a more appropriate comparison? Do the three regions of the Netherlands (with their urban centres of Amsterdam and Rotterdam) make a more consistent economic unit than the three regions at the point of junction between France, Belgium and Germany (with the mini-region of Luxembourg at its notional centre)? How far are the observed differences between countries genuine 'country effects'? Or should better-off and worse-off countries be seen simply as combinations of better-off and worse-off regions?

These questions about the distribution of income within and between regions and countries are of general interest for an analysis of patterns of social and economic life across Europe. The answers will be of value to European and national institutions as they look 'down' to consider the distribution of policy effort and of funding between countries and between regions. They will be of value to regional and national institutions as they look 'up', providing a picture of the overall national and European scenes within which their policies have to be developed.

But this nested geographical perspective raises a crucial question when we turn to the specific issue of poverty. Ever since Peter Townsend's seminal analysis (1979), it has been widely recognised that poverty should be seen as a relative concept (see also Gordon and Townsend, 2000). A European Council Decision expressed the official view in 1984:

> **The poor shall be taken to mean persons ... whose resources (material, cultural and social) are so limited as to exclude them from the minimum acceptable way of life in the Member States in which they live.**

The Council referred to the way of life of 'member states'; and it is on that basis that national median incomes are almost invariably used as the benchmark against which income poverty is measured. But the location of 'country' as a geographical entity in between 'Europe' on the one hand and 'region' on the other opens this convention to enquiry from both directions.

- When national governments measure poverty among their constituent regions, they always use the benchmark derived from the larger (national) unit. Why, then, should European analysis not use a Europe-wide benchmark? The implications of such a shift of perspective are obvious: a Europe-wide poverty line would radically increase the number of poor households in low-income countries such as Portugal and Greece, and virtually wipe out poverty in Luxembourg.

- If the answer to that question is that the concept of exclusion makes sense only in relation to the conditions people see around them, why stop at country – why not use a regional benchmark? Arguably, this would provide greater consistency between small countries and large countries. It would have substantial impact on the estimates of poverty rates in countries with a wide range of inequality between regions.

A number of researchers have acknowledged the relevance of a possible Europe-wide poverty line, but have not gone on to assess the implications in any detail[3]. Hagenaars with others (1998), for example, provide national estimates of the number of poor households using national and EU-wide benchmarks, simply to illustrate the different outcomes. Atkinson (1998) suggests that national and Union-based benchmarks are at opposite ends of a continuum; he argues that a benchmark might be based on some combination of national and EU perspectives, and suggests the formula

$$50\% \text{ of } Y_{EU}^{\theta} . Y_{country}^{(1-\theta)}$$

for calculating a poverty line, in which the Ys are the average incomes of Europe and of the household's country of residence, and θ (theta) is a measure of the relative importance assigned to EU as opposed to national considerations. But, in the absence of any suggested value for the weight, this proposes a way of

thinking about the question without offering a solution.

Note that the Atkinson formulation pushes the benchmark, if anything, towards consideration of the wider European distribution. Part of the argument of the current study is that national averages are not necessarily one end of the continuum, and that the narrower regional averages have, in principle, just as much right to consideration as either of the other geographical units.

Many of these issues have been well discussed by Kangas and Ritakallio (2002). They quote Adam Smith as the authority for a national relative view of poverty:

> By necessity I understand, not only the commodities which are indispensably necessary for the support of life, but whatever the custom of the country renders it indecent for creditable people, even of the lowest order, to be without.... Custom has rendered leather shoes a necessary of life in England. The poorest creditable person of either sex would be ashamed to appear in publick without them. In Scotland, custom has rendered them a necessary of life to the lowest order of men, but not to the same order of women.... In France they are necessaries neither to men nor to women.

Kangas and Ritakallio argue that:

> the deepening European integration creates uniform standards of comparison and common European yard-sticks for the measurement of poverty and level of living. The French are more aware of the quality of English leather shoes.

On the other hand, they say,

> visions of a Europe of regions, ie Europe that has been divided in terms of regional affiliation ... would support distinguishing as units of analysis some further limited regional areas.... To what extent are the Scots really different from the Englishmen?

It is important to note that raising these questions should not be taken to imply any particular answer. The decision to express income in all countries in terms of commonly estimated units of purchasing power immediately leads the analytical eye towards a

---

[3] Blackburn (1998) presents comparisons between countries using a common measure of purchasing power as an 'absolute' measure of poverty, similar in concept to using a fixed real poverty line for comparisons over time within countries. This 'absolute' perspective is appropriate if the countries being compared are theorised as being distinct from each other (in Blackburn's case, the US, Canada, Australia and a selection from Europe). In the current study, the countries of Europe are hypothesised to be members of a single unit, so a common European poverty line would still be interpreted as 'relative'.

commonly defined poverty line in which low-income countries are shown to have a large number of 'poor' households. The regional perspective provides, however, a counterbalance to that way of looking at the issues. The underlying point is that poverty is a relative phenomenon. The question is – relative to where? Should people's purchasing power be compared with that of their immediate neighbours within a region[4], with that of the nation-state of which they are citizens and whose culture they share, or with the European Union with which they share a single market?

These may be largely political issues, depending on people's and politicians' sense of the geographical and administrative unit that most closely expresses their identity. A 'minimum rights' approach to poverty (Atkinson, 1998), for example, is much more concerned with political issues about the range of bottom-inequality that should be tolerated in each society rather than with directly economic issues about levels of consumption. Much of the analysis in this paper simply illustrates the effect of different area perspectives on the poverty estimates in each country. The findings may be of value to those who think that the choice of benchmark should be based on these essentially political considerations, but who need to assess the implications of the alternative approaches.

An alternative view is that the boundaries of the community with which households' incomes are compared should coincide with the administrative unit with the primary responsibility for the relevant sets of policies. Within Europe, that responsibility lies mainly with national governments. In that sense 'country' provides the key reference point. Indeed, it is usually assumed that the combination of each country's historical policy institutions with the actions of recent and current governments

determines the overall extent of poverty in each country. Many analysts have adopted the theoretical framework of 'welfare regimes' (Esping Andersen, 1990, 1999; Ferrara, 1996) to explain why some countries have higher levels of relative poverty than others (Berthoud and Iacovou, 2004). The analysis in Chapter 3 will distinguish four regime types among the 15 European countries: social democratic (Finland, Sweden, Denmark); liberal (UK, Ireland); corporatist (Netherlands, Belgium, Luxembourg, France, Germany, Austria); and residual (Portugal, Spain, Italy, Greece). Countries are listed in that order in all tables to facilitate that comparison, even when it is not explicit in the text.

'Relative to where' may, however, be an empirical question too. We could decide which geographical unit provided the best base for comparison if we understood how the average income of a community affects the point at which (to adapt the words of the 1984 Decision) limited resources lead to exclusion from a community's minimum acceptable way of life. There have been many attempts to define and measure poverty on the basis of direct evidence of social exclusion rather than simply in terms of a low income (Mack and Lansley, 1985; Nolan and Whelan, 1996; Gordon with others, 2000). In this study, income remains the key metric for defining poverty, but two measures of perceived exclusion are used in an attempt to calibrate income-poverty lines in each region and country, to see how sensitive they are to variations in the overall purchasing power of the geographical unit of analysis.

These analyses, in Chapters 7 and 8, may be considered experimental. They are inconclusive, in any case. But they strikingly fail to corroborate the conventional and official view that national boundaries provide the most appropriate base for defining relative incomes.

The objectives of this study, then, are to analyse European household incomes, with an emphasis on variations between and within countries and between and within regions; and to place those variations in the context of the overall distribution of income across the EU. The next chapter (2) deals with methodological and technical points. The following two chapters (3 and 4) analyse first the distribution of household income and then relative poverty, by country. Then a pair of chapters (5 and 6) does the

---

[4] One might argue in principle for shrinking the area of comparison even smaller than the region, to the level of county/department, town or even neighbourhood. The smaller the geographical unit, however, the more likely it is that the income of an area is influenced by the economic position of the people who live there rather than the other way round. At some point, local relativities become misleading, and it seems best to stop at region on theoretical grounds (as well as on the very practical ground that no data are consistently available for units of analysis smaller than the region).

same for income and poverty in regions. Chapters 7
and 8 test two alternative methods of calibrating
poverty lines, to see if they help to answer the key
'relative to where' question. The final chapter draws
conclusions about the geographical distribution of
income and of poverty among the current
membership of the EU, and then briefly raises
questions about the implications of the findings for
the soon-to-be-expanded community.

A glossary of technical terms and abbreviations is
available at Appendix A.

Data from the European Community Household Panel survey

The ECHP

All of the detailed analysis in this study is based on the European Community Household Panel survey (ECHP). The ECHP was designed as a harmonised set of purpose-built surveys covering the whole of the European Union. In principle (the exceptions are noted below) the same set of questions was asked of a random sample of households and of individuals in every country – covering a wide range of subjects including household income and living standards. Members of the sample have been re-interviewed each successive year (thus making it a 'panel' survey), and this means that the data can be used either 'cross-sectionally' to describe the position at any one time or 'longitudinally' to analyse changes from year to year. Each country submits its data to Eurostat, which is responsible for checking that the variables are as far as possible consistent with each other and for deriving summary variables (such as total household income). (For a more detailed description of the survey, see Wirtz and Mejer, 2002.)

The ECHP was launched in 1994 and the final wave of interviews was in 2001. The analysis here is based on the 1999 data, the latest year available at the time of analysis. Analysis was confined to households providing income data. The sample totals around 62,000 households across Europe, ranging from more than 6,000 in Italy to just under 1,000 in Luxembourg (Table 2.1 overleaf).

In fact, the standard pattern of data collection summarised above was true of only nine of the 15 EU countries. The six variations were as follows:

- *The Netherlands* and *Belgium* provided data from existing household panel surveys – the Dutch Socio-Economic Panel (ISEP) and the Panel Study of Belgian Households (PSBH) – which were transcribed into the ECHP format. This means that the data are not always fully consistent with the true ECHP. A number of questions have been raised about the reliability of the income data in the Belgian ECHP file.

- *Sweden* provided data from the Swedish Living Conditions Survey (ULF). The source was not a panel survey, so no longitudinal analysis is possible. It did not ask the questions about perceptions analysed in Chapters 7 and 8, so Sweden is omitted from that analysis.

- *Germany* and the *UK* ran the true ECHP for three years (1994-96). They then switched to data derived from their existing household panel surveys (GSOEP and BHPS). The analysis here uses the 1999 data from the latter surveys, but is obliged to go back to the original ECHP data of 1996 for the analysis of perceptions in Chapters 7 and 8. Income levels for that analysis have been inflated to 1999 levels using factors derived from the GSOEP and BHPS. A shortcoming is that the original ECHP data for Germany do not identify regions, and that country had to be omitted from the regional analysis of perceptions.

- *Luxembourg's* data for 1994-96 were transcribed from one existing panel survey (PSELL-I); the data for 1997 on were derived from a different survey (PSELL-II), but this did not include income data. The analysis of Luxembourg in this study is based on the 1996 survey, with income amounts inflated to 1999 rates by a factor derived from the national accounts.

Table 2.1: Number of households in each country's sample

	Analysis of income (chs 3 to 7)	Analysis of perceptions (chs 7 and 8)
Finland	3,822	
Sweden	5,165	none
Denmark	2,387	
UK	4,951	3,775
Ireland	2,378	
Netherlands	5,023	
Belgium	2,712	
Luxembourg	933	
France	5,610	
Germany	5,847	4,593
Austria	2,815	
Portugal	4,683	
Spain	5,418	
Italy	6,370	
Greece	3,986	

Note: See text for an explanation of the different sample numbers in Sweden, the UK and Germany. Centred numbers apply to both sets of analyses.

Weighting

The analysis here is derived entirely from the ECHP household file, augmented by summary data about countries supplied by Eurostat. The raw data for each household were weighted by a factor that addressed two objectives: balancing the sample *within* each country, and balancing the sample *between* countries.

Eurostat supplies a weighting factor that it has calculated to make the data for each country as representative as possible. Its calculation has been based on:

- counteracting deliberate variations in the initial sampling fraction between regions within each country;
- correcting for deviations in the composition of the initial sample in comparison with known data about the age and sex structure of the country's population; and
- correcting for variations in attrition since the initial wave of interviews.

In fact Eurostat's highly detailed calculation produces a very wide range of household weights – at the extreme, the ratio of the highest to the lowest weight in Germany is 2,690:1. Weighting has an adverse

effect on the accuracy of estimates based on sample data; and the wider the range of weights, the more serious the effect. So the analysis in this study used a much simplified weighting matrix. Within each country, households were ordered from lowest income to highest income and then divided into 10 equal groups (decile groups). The average Eurostat weight for each decile group within each region was calculated, and it was this average, rather than individual household weights, that was applied to the data. Since the averaging took account of variations between income groups and between regions – the two key dimensions of the analysis – the results were very similar to those that would have been obtained using individual household weights, but less sensitive to sampling error. The widest range of weights, still in Germany, was now down to 6.3:1.

Many analysts also weight the data by the number of individuals living in each household, to provide, in effect, person-based estimates of the prevalence of poverty. Such a weight makes little difference to the overall conclusions of the analysis in this paper. Since it adds to sampling error without improving accuracy in other ways, it was judged to be an unnecessary complication and was not applied.

A second weighting factor was used to take account of the varying size of the countries included in the ECHP. This was calculated as the total number of households in the country (as estimated by Eurostat) divided by the total number of households in the sample. The use of this weight meant that the average income of the EU (and of other aggregations of countries) was a true average across all households.

When summary data for countries or regions were being cross-analysed, using correlation coefficients or regression equations, the calculations were always weighted by the estimated number of households in each country or region. This meant that the data for large countries such as Germany were given much more weight than those for small countries such as Ireland or Luxembourg.

Choice of income variable

The standard ECHP dataset includes two variables providing distinct estimates of the total income of each household.

One, referred to here as 'current income', is based on asking the householder to provide a single figure for the aggregate income of the whole household during the current week or month. There are two potential disadvantages of this measure:

- It requires the householder to add up all the sources of income of all the household members. If he or she has not calculated this sum before, the mental arithmetic may not be accurate.
- The current week or month may be unusual for some reason, and provide an inaccurate indication of the household's long-run resources.

The other, referred to here as 'annual income', is based on detailed questions asking each member of the household to report the amount of each source of income (earnings, dividends, pensions, social security benefits and so on) received during each month of the calendar year prior to the interview (that is, 1998 for the 1999 survey). There are four potential disadvantages of this measure:

- It requires each respondent to remember the amount of each source of income they received during each month of the previous year. It is extremely unlikely that people whose income varies from month to month could do that with any accuracy, unless they looked up the detailed record.
- The raw data have to be heavily processed by Eurostat, first to allocate country-specific sources of income to standard categories, and second to estimate (impute) elements of the household income that had not been reported. Even if Eurostat's calculations are assumed to be the best possible solution to these problems, there is a big gap between the original data supplied by informants and the final variable available for analysis.
- The individuals who make up the household at the time of the interview are not necessarily the same as those who lived together during the previous year, and there may also have been changes in household composition over the course of that year. Data on last year's income received by this year's household members does not represent the true position of the household or of its members, at either point in time.
- Attempts to cross-analyse income with other household characteristics, including the

householder's perceptions (see Chapters 7 and 8), are potentially complicated by the fact that the two sets of variables refer to different time periods.

Official Eurostat analysis of the income data uses the annual income measure because the two disadvantages of the current income variable are deemed to be more important than the four disadvantages of annual income. Most academic analysts follow suit, usually without assessing the relative merits of the two versions. Some comparisons between them are discussed in Appendix B; this analyst is by no means certain that the annual income measure is superior. Nevertheless, all the analysis in Chapters 3 to 6 is based on annual income, simply to maintain consistency with other research. The cross-analysis of income with perceptions in Chapters 7 and 8 has, however, used current income because a much better fit was obtained.

The income variables represent total net household income – that is, including social security benefits and other transfers, and after deduction of direct taxes. Income in kind and imputed rent are not included. The data refer to the period before the introduction of the Euro; amounts recorded in units of national currency have been converted to a common scale using the purchasing power parities supplied by Eurostat. The unit of account is 'purchasing power standards' (PPS), which can be thought of as the quantity of goods and services that could be bought for one dollar in the country concerned. As it happens, the ECU (later to become the Euro) was roughly equivalent to a dollar in 1999, so the PPS can be thought of as similar to a Euro.

Net household incomes have been adjusted for household size using the modified OECD equivalence scale (1.0 for a single adult + 0.5 for each additional adult + 0.3 for each child).

Index of inequality

A wide variety of statistics can be calculated to summarise inequality of incomes within an area (Jenkins, 1991; Cowell, 1995), each of which focuses on some particular set of characteristics of the distribution. The most well-known is the Gini coefficient. But the Gini cannot measure the relative contributions of inequality *between* countries and *within* countries to the overall inequality across Europe, or compare the contributions of inequality *between* and *within* regions.

The index of inequality chosen to summarise these distributions is the mean logarithmic deviation. Jenkins (1999) explains that this is one of a family of generalised entropy indices, GE(*a*). These indices differ in their sensitivities to income differences in different parts of the distribution. The more positive *a* is, the more sensitive GE(*a*) is to income differences at the top of the distribution; the more negative *a* is, the more sensitive the index is to differences at the bottom of the distribution. GE(1) is known as the Theil index. The mean logarithmic deviation is GE(0); it was selected for this study because it provided the closest association between the measure of overall inequality and the relative poverty rate in the 15 countries. It is calculated as the mean value of:

$$\text{Log}_n \frac{\text{Mean income}}{\text{Individual income}}$$

It can be additively decomposed as:

$$\text{GE}(0)_{\text{overall}} = \text{GE}(0)_{\text{between-group}} + \text{GE}(0)_{\text{within-group}}$$

and this means that the contributions of between-country or between-region differences can be calculated as a percentage of overall EU inequality.

This approach to a comparison of within- and between-country income inequalities is very similar to that adopted by Beblo and Knau (2001) in their analysis of incomes in 'Euroland'.

The calculation is referred to as the *inequality index* throughout this study. It is compared with the Gini coefficient in Table 3.1. It can be seen there that the selected inequality index for countries tends to be about 0.13 points lower than the Gini coefficient, but that the differences between countries are very similar according to both measures.

3

Income variations between (and within) countries

The average net equivalent household income in the European Union was about 14,000 PPS in 1999. It is not the aim of the current analysis to compare that EU average with other blocks of countries, although part of the argument is that the Union does have a meaningful overall average on which would it be appropriate to base such a comparison. The intention on this occasion is to show how the income is distributed among the 150 million households within Europe. The range of household incomes – between the first and the 99th percentiles – is from 1,500 PPS to 44,500 PPS: a ratio of 1:30. The distribution across all households is illustrated by the rising and falling curve in Figure 3.a – a classic skewed normal-income distribution with a steep increase in the number of households across the range 1,500-11,000 PPS, and an elongated tail of households with substantially higher incomes.

The smooth rising curve in Figure 3.a presents the same distribution of incomes across households

Figure 3.a: Distribution of annual net equivalent household incomes across households and across countries in the EU

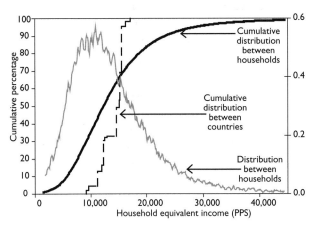

cumulatively – it shows the proportion of households with up to a given income. Again, the long distorted S is the standard shape of cumulative household income distributions.

The jagged vertical line shows the cumulative distribution of income across countries, weighted by the number of households in each country. In effect, this shows what the distribution across households would look like if each were assumed to have the average income of its country. It is instantly clear that the range of incomes between countries is much narrower than the range between households. The first and 99th percentiles of the weighted distributions between countries are 9,100 PPS and 17,100 PPS: a ratio of about 1:2. This narrower range of incomes between countries is logically obvious, but it helps to place analysis of income variations between countries in context. The inequality index described in Chapter 2 suggests that the contribution of inequality between countries to the overall range of inequality between households in Europe is only 5.5%:

Index of inequality across all households in the EU	0.183
Index of inequality across households *within* countries	0.173
Index of inequality *between* countries	0.010
Between-country inequality as a proportion of overall inequality	5.5%

While the overall range of Euro-variation in household incomes can be divided into a between-country (0.010) and a within-country (0.173) component, within-country inequality can also vary between countries. The index of within-country inequality ranges from 0.12 in Denmark to 0.25 in

Table 3.1: Inequality in annual net equivalent household income, within countries

	Median annual income (PPS)	Inequality index (see ch 2)	Gini coefficient	Regime type
Finland	10,782	0.17	0.30	Social democratic
Sweden	10,724	0.13	0.25	
Denmark	15,658	0.12	0.25	
UK	12,287	0.21	0.33	Liberal
Ireland	10,593	0.21	0.34	
Netherlands	13,464	0.14	0.27	Corporatist
Belgium	13,878	0.18	0.31	
Luxembourg	22,816	0.15	0.29	
France	13,223	0.16	0.30	
Germany	13,757	0.14	0.27	
Austria	13,815	0.16	0.29	
Portugal	7,275	0.25	0.38	Residual
Spain	9,352	0.21	0.33	
Italy	10,975	0.17	0.30	
Greece	7,766	0.24	0.36	

Note: Standard errors of the median and the inequality index are presented in Appendix D, Table D1.

Portugal (Table 3.1, centre column)[5]. On this evidence, Portugal is twice as unequal as Denmark.

Analysts' first instinct would be to look for an explanation of these differences in terms of the social policy regimes of the countries (last column of Table 3.1) – the social democratic regimes should promote greater equality, the liberal and residual regimes would be expected to allow greater inequality (Esping-Andersen, 1990). Figure 3.b uses different symbols to represent the four regimes when the countries' indices of inequality are plotted, but also takes account of the overall position of the countries on the European income ladder. Much the most striking finding is that the inequality index is inversely related to median income: low-income countries have more inequality and high-income countries have less inequality. Regime type seems less important, although it remains true that the UK's exceptionally wide range of inequality is consistent with its 'liberal' approach, while Sweden's exceptionally low level of inequality is consistent with its membership of the 'social democratic' group.

Another potential source of variation between countries is the location of the main inequalities. Is the gap in incomes bigger at the bottom of the scale or at the top? Figure 3.c compares countries on two measures: the ratios of the 10th percentile (lowest decile) to the median and the ratio of the 90th percentile (highest decile) to the median (represented by the lower and upper lines of symbols respectively).

Figure 3.b: Within-country inequality plotted against country median income

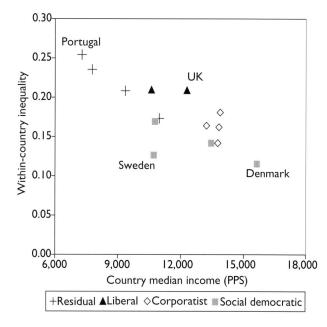

Note: Luxembourg, not shown, would appear off the chart to the right.

---

[5] Gini coefficients, which are more familiar to many readers, are shown in the right-hand column of the table. The pattern of variation between countries is almost identical, whichever of the two measures of inequality is used.

Figure 3.c: 10th and 90th percentiles of household income relative to the median, by country

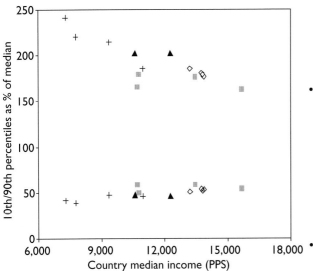

Note: Symbols indicate welfare regimes using the same key as in Figure 3.b. Luxembourg, not shown, would appear off the chart to the right.

- The 10th percentile indicates the lowness of low incomes: there is a slight tendency for countries with low overall positions in the European income scale to report low-income levels that are even worse. The 10th percentile is only 42% of the median in Portugal, but as high as 54% in Denmark. Thus 'low-inequality' is somewhat wider in low-income countries.
- The 90th percentile indicates the highness of high incomes: here there is a strong tendency for countries with low overall positions in the European scale to report high-income levels that are rather higher than might have been expected. The 90th percentile ranges from 241% of the median in Portugal, to 163% in Denmark. So 'high-inequality' is much wider in low-income countries.
- One of the consequences of this pattern of inequalities is that the absolute gap in purchasing power between the relatively well-off people in each country is much narrower than the gap between relatively poor people in each country. Low-income households in Denmark have 2.8 times as much income as those in Portugal; high-income households in Denmark have an advantage of only 1.5 times. This conclusion will have important implications for our analysis, in the next chapter, of household poverty.

	Denmark	Portugal	Ratio D/P
10th percentile	8,495	3,065	2.8
90th percentile	25,474	17,561	1.5

4

National relative poverty

One of the aims of this analysis is to see how this pattern of income inequality within and between countries changes when we look at *regions* within each country. First, however, the analysis remains with the 15 countries of Europe for detailed consideration of national poverty rates. Throughout most of this chapter, poverty is defined relatively. Various definitions of poverty will be used, but they are based in one way or another on a comparison of the income of each household with the distribution of income within the country where the household lives. Variations in living standards between countries (as recorded in Table 3.1) are not initially taken into account in deciding which households are poor, although they will be taken into account in analysing which countries have high and low relative poverty rates. Only at the very end of the chapter (Table 4.2)

do income variations between countries influence the estimates of poverty rates.

Although various relative poverty thresholds have been calculated over the years (for example, 40%, 50% or 60% of the mean, 50%, 60% or 70% of the median), the version that is now most often used, and officially adopted by the European Council at its Laeken summit, is 60% of the national median (Atkinson with others, 2002). The average poverty rate across the EU on that measure is 16%, ranging from a low of 10.8% in Sweden to a high of 22.8% in Portugal. The summary in the right-hand column of Table 4.1 shows that poverty rates are on average lower in the three countries said to have a social democratic social policy regime, and higher in the four countries with residual regimes – but individual countries within those groups depart from that general pattern.

The analysis of income variations within countries (Figure 3.b) showed, however, that countries with low overall levels of income also suffered from high rates of internal inequality. Figure 4.a (the black diamonds[6]) shows that relative poverty is also more common in low-income countries – this follows almost inevitably from the earlier conclusion about inequality rates. There is a clear gradation between low-income Portugal, with its high rate of relative poverty, and high-income Denmark, with very little relative poverty. It needs to be said again that these are relative poverty rates, and the link between national income and relative poverty rates does not flow directly from the variations in the countries' overall standards of living.

Table 4.1: National poverty rates using the 60% of median threshold (%)

	Poverty rate in country	Average poverty rate by regime type	
Finland	16.0	Social democratic	12.7
Sweden	10.8		
Denmark	13.3		
UK	19.4	Liberal	19.5
Ireland	22.7		
Netherlands	10.9	Corporatist	14.2
Belgium	14.1		
Luxembourg	12.2		
France	16.1		
Germany	13.4		
Austria	15.4		
Portugal	22.8	Residual	18.5
Spain	17.8		
Italy	17.7		
Greece	21.1		

Note: Standard errors of the poverty rates are presented in Appendix D, Table D1.

---

[6] The hollow circles in Figure 4.b are discussed on page 15.

Figure 4.a: National relative poverty rates, plotted against national median incomes

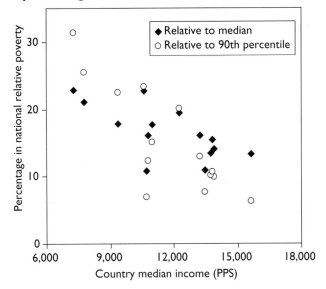

The correlation between national median income and national relative poverty rates (weighted by the number of households in each country) is 0.74. This can be thought of as a measure of the straightness of the slope linking the black diamonds in Figure 4.a. A simple regression equation (also weighted) calculates that the poverty rate in a country with a median income of 7,000 PPS would be 21.6%, and that the rate falls by 1.0 percentage point for every 1,000 PPS increase in the national median.

It is often argued that poverty rates based on calculations of income in a single year may be too sensitive to temporary changes in households' circumstances (Whelan with others, 2003). One suggestion is to extend the period of measurement. Here the panel data from the ECHP have been used to define the 'persistent poor' as individuals whose household income fell below 60% of the national median three years running at some stage over a five-year period. The proportion in persistent poverty ranged from 3% in Denmark to 20% in Portugal[7]. The weighted correlation between national median income and the persistent poverty rate rises to 0.81. That is, the relationship is even stronger for persistent poverty than for annual poverty.

Another way of reconsidering relative poverty is to vary the benchmark within the national income distribution against which incomes are compared. The convention is to use the median, representing a central reference point with as many households above it as below it. One of the reasons for using the median rather than the mean as the national reference point is that the mean takes account of the riches of the rich, and it has been argued that these are not relevant to a consideration of the lifestyle of the poor. The principal theorist of relative deprivation argued that people tended to compare their positions with those of their immediate neighbours in time, space and the socio-economic hierarchy (Runciman, 1966). An alternative argument, on the contrary, is that upper incomes should be the main reference point. After all, it is the lifestyle of upper-income groups that is mainly portrayed on television and in the newspapers. Most of the academics who calibrate poverty lines are in the upper-income range; so are the journalists who comment on them and the politicians who determine anti-poverty policies. So it would be legitimate to propose an alternative poverty line set at 30% of the 90th percentile, rather than 60% of the 50th percentile (median). Since 90th percentiles are typically about double the median, this alternative gives a similar poverty rate across Europe as a whole: 14.6% for the 30/90 poverty line, compared with 16.2% for the 60/50 line. Note that poverty is still defined here in terms of the internal distribution of income within each country – entirely relative.

Remember, though, the systematic differences between the high- and low-income countries in the extent of 'high-inequality' – see Figure 3.c. We know that 90th percentiles are substantially higher in relation to the median in low-income countries such as Portugal than in high-income countries such as Denmark. This means that transferring the relative poverty benchmark to the 90th percentile has important implications for the poverty count across countries. The poverty rate rises from 23% to 31% in Portugal. It falls from 13% to 6% in Denmark. The new estimates are illustrated as the hollow circles in Figure 4.a. The relationship between national median incomes and 30/90 poverty is much steeper than it was for the standard 60/50 definition. The weighted correlation coefficient rises from 0.74 to 0.84.

---

[7] Thanks to Richard Layte of the Economic and Social Research Institute, Dublin, for supplying these calculations of persistent poverty. They are based on the 1994-98 sequence, and confined to the 11 countries contributing to all five waves.

Table 4.2: National poverty rates: three benchmarks compared (%)

	National benchmarks		EU benchmark
	60% of median	30% of 90th percentile	60% of median
Finland	16.0	12.3	22.3
Sweden	10.8	6.9	16.8
Denmark	13.3	6.3	5.7
UK	19.4	20.1	19.5
Ireland	22.7	23.3	31.7
Netherlands	10.9	7.6	8.3
Belgium	14.1	9.9	9.9
Luxembourg	12.2	11.5	1.9
France	16.1	12.9	13.0
Germany	13.4	10.2	9.9
Austria	15.4	10.7	10.6
Portugal	22.8	31.3	51.2
Spain	17.8	22.4	34.5
Italy	17.7	15.0	23.4
Greece	21.1	25.5	46.4

These revised poverty rates based on comparing household incomes with the 90th percentile are recorded in the centre column of Table 4.2, where it can be seen that there are substantial differences in the proportion of households judged to be poor, depending on which benchmark is chosen.

The conclusion that national relative poverty rates are systematically higher in countries with low overall average incomes is important; it is unexpected in the sense that it is not a direct outcome of the definition of poverty. If the poverty line is based, instead, on reference to a single European benchmark, then the change of definition automatically increases the number of poor households found in the low-income countries and reduces the number found in the high-income countries. The third column of Table 4.2 illustrates this: the proportion of households in Euro-poverty increases to 51% and 46% in Portugal and Greece, and falls to 2% and 6% in Luxembourg and Denmark. This perspective hugely increases the apparent importance of poverty in southern European countries. It reduces the extent of poverty in many northern European countries. But, because there are some large countries with fairly high poverty rates in the north (such as the UK), a substantial proportion of poor households is still observed in the north.

5

Income variations between (and within) regions

The analysis so far has set income variations between European countries in the context of income variations between households within countries. But the variation between households within a country can also be partitioned geographically, and it is important to take account of inequality within and between regions[8]. This is partly because regional variations within countries are of interest in their own right. It will be seen, for example, that the range of regional inequality across Italy is much wider than it is across the UK.

In the European context, however, regions are also an important element in the assessment of variations between countries. Do variations between countries actually represent country effects, or are they simply regional variations that happen to aggregate to countries? Are the differences between small neighbouring countries (such as Finland and Sweden) equivalent to the differences between large countries, or should they be interpreted as more akin to variations between neighbouring regions within a large country? Is it more appropriate to compare the north of France with the nearby Walloon (French-speaking) region of Belgium, or with the Midi, in the same country but a thousand kilometres away?

In principle, geographical variations can be nested in a hierarchical structure, moving successively from Europe, down through countries, regions, municipal districts, neighbourhoods and streets. Measuring fine-grained local variations across 15 countries is well beyond the reach of a general purpose survey such as the ECHP, although such analysis within individual countries can be based on specialised surveys (Berthoud, 2001). It is, however, possible to take account of regional variations, so that households can be aggregated to regions, and regions to countries.

The practical difficulty is in defining regions in ways that are broadly comparable across countries. Eurostat has assembled the regional classification systems used by each national statistical office in a sequence known as the Nomenclature of Territorial Units for Statistics (NUTS). The analysis here uses the broadest regional classification available in each country (NUTS1) as its starting point. But even here, smaller countries naturally tend to divide their populations into relatively small regions, and it is necessary to regroup regions so that the units in each country are of broadly comparable size. The regrouping is summarised in Table 5.1; more details are shown in Appendix C. The principles were as follows:

- In the five large countries, most of the original NUTS1 regions were allowed to stand. Regions containing fewer than one million households were, however, merged with an immediate neighbour.
- In six medium-sized countries, original regions were combined in order to average about two million households per grouped region. Groupings were of neighbouring regions, and

---

8 The word 'region' is always used here to mean sub-divisions of countries (for example, South East Spain compared with North West Spain; it is not used in its alternative sense of groups of countries (for example, the Mediterranean region compared with the Scandinavian region). Another linguistic complication is that the UK consists of four 'countries' (England, Wales, Scotland and Northern Ireland); in this study, Scotland, Wales and Northern Ireland are treated as regions of the UK, equivalent in size to the regions of England.

Table 5.1: Summary of regional groupings

Country	Number of original regions	Number of region-groups	Number of households in region-groups (millions)		
			Average	Smallest	Largest
Five large countries					
UK	12	10	2.4	1.9	3.7
France	8	8	3.0	1.5	4.5
Germany	16	12	3.1	1.1	8.2
Spain	7	6	2.1	1.4	3.8
Italy	11	9	2.4	1.6	3.6
Six medium countries					
Sweden	8	2	2.3	2.2	2.3
Netherlands	4	3	2.2	1.1	3.2
Belgium	3	2	2.1	1.8	2.4
Austria	3	2	1.6	1.5	1.8
Portugal	7	2	1.6	1.6	1.7
Greece	4	2	1.9	1.9	2.0
Three small countries					
Finland	5	1	2.4	2.4	2.4
Denmark	1	1	2.4	2.4	2.4
Ireland	2	1	1.3	1.3	1.3
One tiny country					
Luxembourg	1	0	na	na	na
All Europe	92	61	2.5	1.1	8.2

Note: The number of households in each region was estimated by grossing up the weighted ECHP survey data, using grossing factors derived from the number of households in the country. Sample sizes and standard errors for the regional analysis are available in Appendix D, Table D2.

small regions were grouped rather than large ones. Some of the groupings may be considered rather arbitrary, but it should be noted that the analysis is not really so concerned with estimating the income of any particular region as with the role of 'regions' in the overall European pattern of inequality.

- Three small countries were each treated as consisting of a single region.
- Luxembourg is so much smaller than any of the regions of other countries that it was not treated as a 'region' at all in the analysis by region – although it was, of course, treated as a country in the country analysis.

The main objective of this grouping was to achieve roughly the same average size of region in each of the 14 countries with substantial populations. This improves the comparability of the regional analysis. It should be stressed, however, that these regions cannot be interpreted as providing an 'ideal' or absolute measure of the position of middle-size geographical units in the distribution of income. A standard principle of spatial analysis is the 'modifiable areal units problem' (Openshaw, 1977, summarised in Johnston with others, 1994). It has been shown that, if all possible ways of dividing a space into geographical units are tested, all possible statistical outcomes can be observed. Any particular delineation of units has to be regarded as essentially arbitrary unless it has been based on an empirical analysis designed to optimise the groupings with respect to the variable of interest (in this case, income). Not only are the regions of Europe defined in an arbitrary way; they have been defined in a different arbitrary way by each of the countries concerned. The analyst simply has to accept them as they are.

The median incomes of each region are mapped in Figure 5.a and illustrated graphically in Figure 5.b on page 20. The poorest region in Europe (as just defined) is mainland Greece, with a median annual net household equivalent income of 6,568 PPS; the

Figure 5.a: EU regions plotted by median income

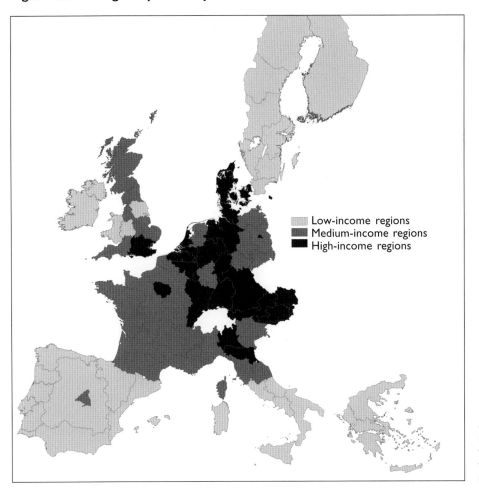

Low-income regions
Medium-income regions
High-income regions

Note: The three shadings represent the bottom third, the middle third and the top third of regions by median net equivalent household income.

most prosperous is the Ile de France, whose median is 16,694 PPS[9]. So the range of incomes between regions is rather wider than between countries (7,275 to 15,658 if Luxembourg is omitted) – as it logically had to be. The index of between-region inequality is 0.017 (compared with 0.010 for between-country inequality).

Greece and France are not the poorest and richest countries, and the fact that they contain the poorest and richest regions illustrates the importance of variations between regions within countries. The two regions of Greece are much more widely spaced than any of the other two-region countries (Figure

5.b). Among the large countries, France is characterised by having a single relatively rich region, with all other regions closely grouped at a lower level. The UK is similar, except that there are two rich regions, followed by a group of less prosperous ones. Spain's and Italy's regions are widely spaced; Germany's are quite tightly grouped.

Table 5.2 overleaf provides details of the regional variations observed in the five largest countries. The capital cities London, Paris (Ile de France) and Madrid are all the richest regions in their respective countries, although Berlin and Rome (Lazio) are not. In Italy the North clearly dominates the South; in the UK the South East dominates the rest of the country; in Germany, the regions of East Germany are clustered towards the lower end of the regional distribution.

9   Mainland Greece – this excludes Attica (the region containing Athens) as well as the islands. Ile de France is the region containing Paris.

Figure 5.b: Median regional net household equivalent incomes

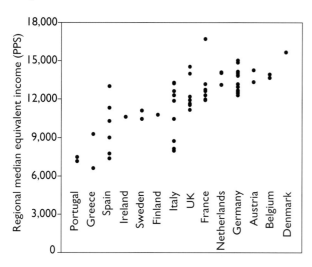

Note: Countries are ordered by their national median income, but spaced equally along the horizontal axis. Values and standard errors of the median incomes are presented in Appendix D, Table D2.

The extent of these regional variations within the five large countries is summarised in Table 5.3 overleaf, which uses the index of inequality that has already been used to summarise variations between countries. The UK and Spain have similar ranges of overall inequality, but in Spain twice as much of that variation can be explained in terms of regional factors. Italy shows much the widest variation between regions, both absolutely and in relation to the overall national picture; Germany has much the narrowest range of variation between regions – one sixth of the Italian figure.

The wide *regional* variations in Spain and Italy have further implications for our interpretation of inequality between *countries*. Each of these countries could be divided in two: a prosperous half on a par with the other developed economies to the north, and a low-income half on a par with the two poorest countries, Portugal and Greece (return to Figures 5.a and 5.b). The same distinction can be seen to divide

Table 5.2: Regional median incomes in relation to country medians: the five large countries

Country median = 100

UK		France		Germany		Spain		Italy	
London	118	Ile de France	126	Hesse	109	Madrid	139	Lombardy	121
South East England	114	East	100	Bavaria	108	North East	121	Emilia-Romagna	120
Scotland	99	Central East	99	Berlin	103	East	110	North East	115
North West England	97	Mediterranean	96	Schleswig-Holstein/Hamburg	102	North West	96	North West	112
South West England	95	Bassin Parisien	96	North Rhine-Westphalia	101	South/Canaries	82	Central	108
East Midlands/East Anglia	94	West	93	Lower Saxony/Bremen	101	Central	79	Lazio	95
North England	94	South West	90	Baden-Wurttemberg	101			Abruzzo-Molise/Campania	79
Northern Ireland/Wales	94	North – Pas-de-Calais	90	Rhineland Palatinate/Saarland	95			South	74
West Midlands	94			Saxony-Anhalt	94			Sicily/Sardinia	73
Yorkshire and Humberside	91			Brandenburg/Mecklenburg-West Pomerania	92				
				Saxony	90				
				Thuringia	89				

Note: Regions are listed in order of median income. Where two original regions have been grouped, their names are separated by a forward slash (/). Values and standard errors of the median incomes are presented in Appendix D, Table D2.

Table 5.3: Measures of inequality within and between regions: the five large countries

	UK	France	Germany	Spain	Italy
Index of inequality across all households in the country	0.209	0.164	0.142	0.208	0.173
Index of inequality across households *within* regions	0.202	0.154	0.139	0.194	0.155
Index of inequality *between* regions	0.007	0.010	0.003	0.014	0.018
Between-region inequality as a proportion of overall inequality	3.4%	6.2%	2.2%	6.6%	10.3%

Note: Values and standard errors of the medians and inequality indices are presented in Appendix D, Table D2.

Europe in two, with the low-income south including not only the four regions of Portugal and Greece but also the six poorest regions of Spain and Italy.

Within-region inequality is mapped in Figure 5.c. Of course the range of variations between households within each region is far wider than the range between regions – as Table 5.3 confirms. Figure 5.d (overleaf) plots within-region inequality, on exactly the same basis as Figure 3.c did for within-country inequality. The pattern is the same, with rich regions showing a much narrower range of household incomes than poor regions. Mainland Greece and Denmark (the whole of Denmark seen on this occasion as a region) are exactly where they should be, with high and low inequality indices respectively. The outliers are interesting, however. The three regions with the widest range of internal inequality (after their median income has been taken into account) are London, Madrid and Ile de France

Figure 5.c: EU regions plotted by degree of inequality

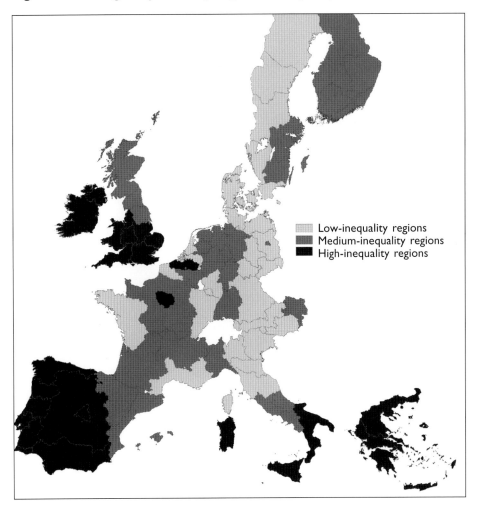

Low-inequality regions
Medium-inequality regions
High-inequality regions

Note: The three shadings represent the bottom third, the middle third and the top third of regions by inequality index.

– the three capital cities that are also exceptionally dominant within their countries. The five regions with unexpectedly low levels of inequality are the northern half of Sweden and four of the five non-Berlin regions of East Germany[10]. These comparisons suggest that there is also an urban/rural influence on income inequalities. Alternatively, the low range of inequality within East Germany might be explained as a residual effect of the former socialist regime there. If so, the regional analysis reveals an effect of social policy regime which was not strongly evident from a comparison between whole countries.

Figure 5.d: Within-region inequality plotted against regional median income

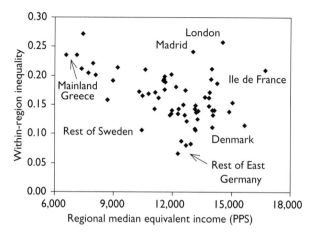

---

[10] The four data points labelled 'rest of East Germany' are Brandenburg, Saxony, Saxony-Anhalt and Thuringia.

6

Regional relative poverty

These conclusions about the distribution of income within and between regions have some clear implications for the analysis of poverty by region. It is important, however, to think carefully about the framework of comparison for setting poverty lines for regional analysis. The convention is to compare every household's income with the median for the *country* in which it lives. This assumes that the normal daily life from which the poor are excluded is based on national identities – the Irish comparing themselves with 'normal' Irish households, the Germans comparing themselves with 'normal' German households (to take the smallest and the largest of the countries – other than Luxembourg – as examples). That might indeed be the most appropriate comparison, but an alternative view is

that, if poverty is really relative, it should be based on a geographical entity that is more consistent in size. If the Irish frame of reference is the other one million or so households in Ireland, maybe Saxons should compare themselves with Saxony, Bavarians with Bavaria, and so on. The analysis in this chapter starts with *regionally* defined poverty lines, moves on to show what happens to the poverty count in each region as the frame of reference moves from region to country, and then moves on to Europe as a whole.

If we use the regional median income as the benchmark, the overall proportion of European households below the regional poverty line is 15.8% – very close to the estimate of 16.2% for national poverty lines. The highest poverty rate, in the

Table 6.1: Variations in poverty rates between regions: four poverty lines compared

	Regional benchmarks		National benchmarks	EU benchmark
	60% of median	30% of 90th percentile	60% of median	60% of median
Highest poverty rate (%)	South Portugal/ Islands	South Portugal/ Islands	Sicily/ Sardinia	Mainland Greece
	23	35	37	57
Lowest poverty rate (%)	Saxony	Thuringia	Emilia-Romagna	Schleswig-Holstein/ Hamburg
	8	2	8	6
Regression equations				
In a country and region with median incomes both at the EU median (13,000 PPS) (%)	14.5	10.9	15.0	13.7
For each additional 1,000 in the *country*'s median income (%)	−1.1	−2.6	−1.2	−5.9
For each additional 1,000 in the *region*'s median income, compared with the country median (%)	0.0	−0.5	−4.0	−4.8

Note: A full list of poverty rates (60% of national median) and standard errors is presented in Appendix D, Table D2. A more technical version of the regression equations is in Table D3.

southern half of Portugal, is quite similar to the national rate in the same country (Table 6.1, first column). The lowest rate, however, in Saxony, is much lower than the national rate in Germany, and this may be associated with the very low levels of inequality observed within the regions of East Germany.

At first sight it appeared that regions with high absolute levels of purchasing power (as measured by the median income in PPS) had low rates of internal poverty – the correlation coefficient between the two measures is –0.38. But it turns out that it is the purchasing power of the country as a whole that is associated with regional poverty rates (a correlation of –0.51) – the median income of the region has no further effect once national incomes have been taken account. The proportion of households in regional poverty falls by 1.0% for each 1,000 PPS increase in the national median.

The second column of Table 6.1 repeats the analysis of relative regional poverty, using this time a poverty line defined as 30% of the 90th percentile instead of 60% of the median. The results are very similar, but all the effects are stronger. The range between the highest and the lowest regional poverty rates is wider; and the association with the overall income level of the country is stronger (the correlation coefficient increases to –0.63).

The relative poverty rates in the first two columns of Table 6.1 have been calculated with the *regional* distribution of income as the benchmark. Most analyses, however, take benchmarks from the *national* income distribution. For single-region countries (Finland, Denmark and Ireland), the choice obviously does not matter, but for larger countries, and especially for the five largest countries, it makes a deal of difference whether each household is assumed to be comparing its income with its immediate or its farther-flung neighbours. We have already established

Figure 6.a: EU regions plotted by national poverty rates

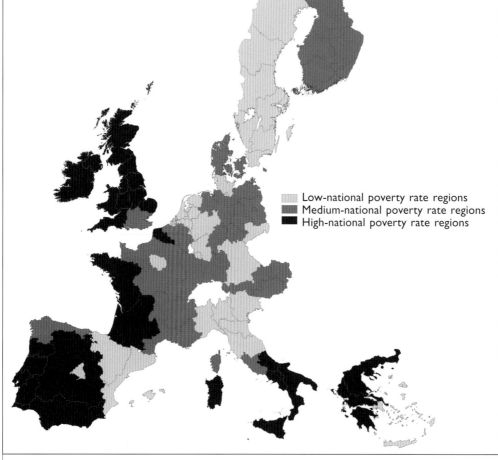

Low-national poverty rate regions
Medium-national poverty rate regions
High-national poverty rate regions

Note: The three shadings represent the bottom third, the middle third and the top third of regions by proportion of households below 60% of the national median.

that relative poverty rates tend to be higher in low-income countries (because such countries have wide ranges of inequality), but it is now logically essential that poverty rates that use national benchmarks will be higher in regions with low incomes – because those are the regions within the country where the poorest people live.

The third column of Table 6.1 calculates regional levels of poverty, based on 60% of the national median. They are mapped in Figure 6.a. The range of rates is substantially wider than was observed when 60% of the regional median was used. Strikingly, both the highest and the lowest poverty rates in Europe occur in the same country – because of the wide range of variation in regional incomes within Italy, recorded in Table 5.3. Regression analysis shows that there is still a tendency for richer countries to show lower regional poverty rates; but that effect is now overshadowed by the systematic tendency for lower-income regions (within each country) to have more poor households.

Figure 6.b: EU regions plotted by Euro-poverty rates

If it makes sense to move from regional benchmarks to national ones, then it is equally logical to see what happens if the EU median is used to define the poverty line. This implies that the poverty line is set at the same level of purchasing power throughout Europe. Whole countries vary in the number of households found to be poor, depending on their national position on the overall income ladder, as already shown in Table 4.2. Regional variations within countries will also have direct effect on the poverty count. The fourth column of Table 6.1, and Figure 6.b, show the outcome: the range of poverty rates widens again, so that fewer than 6% of households in Schleswig-Holstein and Hamburg are poor, but as many as 57% of those in mainland Greece. The latter finding stems directly from the fact that mainland Greece has the lowest income of any region in Europe: in this perspective it is the 'poorest' region in both senses of the word. On the other hand, the richest region in terms of the median purchasing power (Ile de France) is not the least poor in terms of the Euro-poverty rate, because we have seen that the Ile de France, like the other capital cities, has a wider than expected range of within-region inequality.

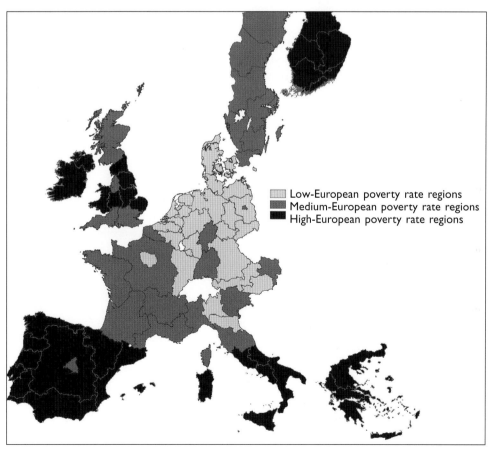

Low-European poverty rate regions
Medium-European poverty rate regions
High-European poverty rate regions

Note: The three shadings represent the bottom, middle and top third of regions by proportion of households below 60% of the Europe-wide median.

7

Calibrating poverty lines according to social norms

The four poverty lines illustrated in Table 6.1 provide very different patterns of variation in poverty rates within and between countries. Is there any way of deciding which is the most appropriate? It was argued in Chapter 1 which there are three ways of addressing that question: a political approach, an institutional approach, and an empirical approach. The empirical approach is to ask what the reference group is against which people perceive themselves or their neighbours to be 'excluded from the minimum acceptable way of life' of their community. This question requires some independent evidence about the relationship between income inequalities and social exclusion in different parts of Europe.

The ECHP survey data provide two possible ways of identifying the level of income associated with social exclusion. This chapter attempts a 'normative' approach to poverty measurement; Chapter 8 tries an alternative approach based on 'financial hardship'. Both approaches are appropriate, although neither is ideal – but they are the best available indicators. The key to both analyses is that, by dividing Europe into regions of roughly equal size, it is possible to compare regional, national and European perspectives. An additional bonus of regional analysis is that there are far more than the 15 units of account to which a country-by-country analysis is necessarily limited.

The first method was originally developed by Dutch and Belgian analysts (Hagenaars, 1986; Deleeck with others, 1992)[11]. It is based on the interview question:

> In your opinion, what is the very lowest net monthly income that your household would have to have in order to make ends meet?

It is not suggested that the answers should be taken at face value, as if those whose income is lower than their own declared minimum should be defined as poor. In the first place, that would be entirely subjective – indeed, this is often referred to as a 'subjective' definition of poverty (Gordon, 2000). In the second place, analysis shows a wide variation in people's estimates of the minimum income they could survive on; and in general, the higher their own income, the higher the minimum they think they require. On the other hand, the perceived minimum increases more slowly than actual income, as illustrated in Figure 7.a. Typically, households low in the income distribution think that they need more than their current income to make ends meet; households high in the income distribution may want more in absolute terms, but they accept that they could make do on less than their current income. It can be suggested that the crossover point is the normative poverty line: the poor cannot argue that

---

[11] The analysis here, however, does not exactly follow the previous researchers' methods of calculating poverty lines; in particular, consistency between this chapter and other analysis in this study required that the standard OECD equivalence scale should be used as an input rather than that poverty lines should be measured separately by household type. See Berthoud and Ford (1996) for a discussion of using subjective data to derive equivalence scales.

Figure 7.a: Stylised representation of the relationship between householders' current income and the minimum they think is needed to make ends meet

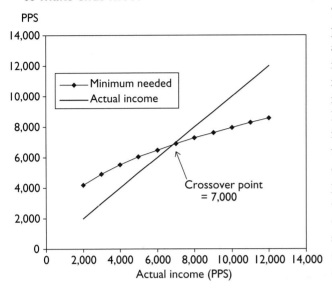

• If all regions and all countries choose a similar norm, that will support the Europe-wide definition of poverty.

The clearest association between actual income and perceived minimum income was found when the analysis used the householder's estimate of current income, rather then the calculated sum of annual income (see page 9 for a discussion of these two income measures). This makes sense because the householder's estimates of actual and minimum income are based on similar mental processes. Both variables were expressed in annual amounts, converted from national currencies to purchasing power standards and equivalised. The regression equation fitted best when both variables were expressed as logarithms (which are much more sensitive to variations at the lower than the upper end of the income distribution). If the regression equation is written:

$$\mathrm{Log}_n(\mathrm{mininc}) = \alpha \times \mathrm{Log}_n(\mathrm{currinc}) + c$$

then the crossover point (where minimum income and current income are the same) can be calculated as:

$$\mathrm{povline}_{norm} = \exp\frac{c}{1-\alpha}$$

Each country's normative poverty line was calculated on the basis of a separate equation, in which both the slope (α) and the constant (c) were allowed to vary between countries. The estimates for regions within countries were based on the country-level equation, in which the slope was fixed for the country, while the constants were allowed to vary between regions – this solution provided more stable results.

Sweden has been omitted from this analysis because its survey does not include the relevant question. The BHPS- and GSOEP-derived versions of the ECHP do not include the question, so the British and German analysis has been based on the third (1996) wave of the original ECHP data instead of the sixth (1999) wave. The income data derived from 1996 has been inflated to 1999 levels using factors derived from the BHPS and GSOEP. The German original ECHP data do not identify regions, so Germany had to be omitted from the regional analysis with the consequent loss of 12 units of analysis.

the line is too low, because it is actually higher than most of them proposed; the rich cannot argue that the line is too high, because it is lower than most of them proposed. Both groups' answers have helped to determine the outcome, which can be interpreted as a norm based on the views of the population of the country or region under consideration.

Whereas the early exponents of this method (Hagenaars, 1986; Deleeck with others, 1992) used it to calculate how many households were 'poor' in relation to this perceived threshold in each country under study, the actual level of the crossover point is not crucial to the current argument (as long as it is not so unreasonably high or low as to suggest that the question has not been answered properly). Once the crossover point has been identified in each country and region, the analysis then needs to compare regional and national variations in the 'normative poverty line' with regional and national variations in purchasing power.

• If there is a strong tendency for richer regions to adopt higher normative lines, that will favour the use of regionally defined poverty thresholds.
• If high-income countries adopt higher normative lines but there is little variation by region within countries, that will favour nationally defined thresholds.

Figure 7.b: Country-level normative poverty lines, plotted by country median income

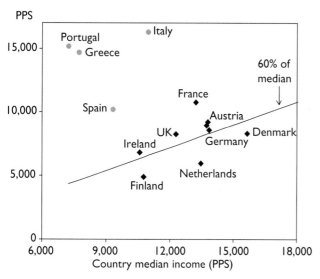

Note: Belgium is the unlabelled country plotted between Austria and Germany. Luxembourg's data (11,600 PPS = 52% of the median) is off the scale to the right. Sweden is omitted.

The normative poverty lines calculated for each country are plotted in Figure 7.b. At first sight the picture is very confusing. National estimates of the minimum income needed to make ends meet range from less than 5,000 PPS (Finland) to more than 16,000 (Italy). Expressed as a proportion of the national median income, the range is between less than half (the Netherlands) and more than double (Portugal). Far from increasing roughly in line with the national average income, the first-sight interpretation of the figure is that normative poverty lines tend to be higher in the countries with *low* averages.

A closer look shows that the four countries in the top-left quadrant of the figure (shown as grey circles) are the four southern countries of Portugal, Greece, Italy and Spain. These countries (with the possible exception of Spain) have agreed on poverty lines so high up the distribution as to lack credibility – in the extreme case, 93% of Portugal's households would be in relative poverty if this evidence were taken at face value. It can be argued that respondents in the

southern countries put a different interpretation on the concept of 'making ends meet'[12].

Eliminating the countries whose data do not fit our theories is a risky business but, if the remaining 10 countries (shown as black diamonds on the graph) are considered on their own, a much more consistent and credible pattern emerges. Now the normative poverty line ranges between 46% of the median (Finland) and 81% (France). In general, it can be seen that higher-income countries tend to have higher agreed poverty lines. Indeed, 60% of the median (drawn as a solid line on the figure) is not a bad approximation to the line of best fit between the (non-southern) countries. The actual calculated line of best fit (based on a regression equation weighted by size of country) is slightly flatter than a fixed proportion of the median: the normative poverty line in a notional country with a median income of zero would be 3,000 PPS, and the line rises by 48 PPS for each 100 increase in the national median (Table 7.1).

Table 7.1: Regression equations explaining country and regional normative poverty lines in terms of country and regional median incomes: excluding southern Europe

	Analysis by country	Analysis by region
Median income of country	0.47	not significant
Median income of region	not applicable	0.68
Constant	2,656	71
Number of observations	10	28
R^2	9.9%	24.4%

Note: For the regional analysis, an initial equation including the median incomes of both region and the country was confined to countries with more than one region. The country-income coefficient was not significant; the equation actually shown included all countries, and omitted country income.

---

[12] Of course 'making ends meet' is the English version, and would have been used directly in only two of the survey questionnaires. It seems unlikely that the north/south split is a directly linguistic one, however: three of the four southern countries use romance languages, which have more in common with the language of France and half of Belgium than with that of Greece.

Figure 7.c: Region-level normative poverty lines excluding southern Europe, plotted by regional median income

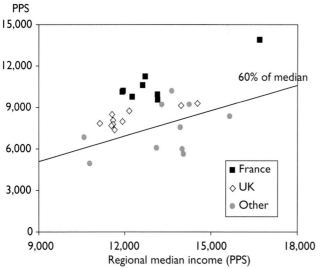

Figure 7.d: Region-level normative poverty lines in southern Europe, plotted by regional median income

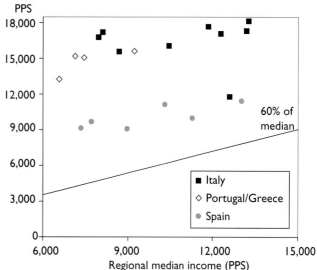

Note: Single-region countries (Finland, Denmark and Ireland) are plotted as regions. Sweden and Germany are omitted.

It is possible to calculate the normative poverty line in each region as well as in each country. Figure 7.c plots the regional poverty lines against the regional median income, with the analysis confined at this stage to the non-southern countries that were found, in Figure 7.b, to behave in a consistent way. Note, however, the absence of a regional analysis for Germany. Within France (black squares), it is clear that respondents in the richest region (Ile de France) have agreed a poverty line substantially higher than those proposed in other regions. Within the UK (white diamonds), the two richest regions (London and South East England) also propose higher than average poverty lines[13]. The regions of the smaller countries of northern and continental Europe (grey circles) align themselves roughly along a trend suggesting higher poverty lines in better-off regions. If we take all the regions in the eight countries covered by Figure 7.c, a weighted regression equation suggests that agreed poverty lines are quite close to a fixed proportion of the regional median income (Table 7.1): a notional region with zero median income would report a normative line of 70 PPS; the poverty line increases by 68 PPS for each 100 PPS of

the regional median income. An important finding, however, is that the median income of the *country* has no effect on variations between *regional* poverty lines, as defined here. On this evidence, it is the regional comparison that matters.

It is worth repeating the warning that the neat relationship between regional incomes and regional poverty lines has been identified only by omitting the countries of southern Europe – effectively on the assumption that respondents in Portugal, Spain, Italy and Greece understood the issues in a different way. Figure 7.d looks at the normative poverty lines in the regions of those four countries. Note that the vertical scale of this graph had to be expanded, compared with Figure 7.c, but the 60% of median line has been included as a common reference point. In Spain, the regional norm is consistently higher than in the northern and continental countries, although it still increases with increasing regional income. Portugal, Italy and Greece are consistent with each other, with normative poverty lines even higher than Spain's[14], although still affected by the incomes of the regions within that group of countries.

---

[13] It might be suggested that the higher requirements in and near the capital cities are based on higher costs of living, especially housing costs, rather than higher consensual standards.

---

[14] With the exception of the North East of Italy, whose normative poverty line is close to the Spanish level.

8

Calibrating poverty lines in terms of the risk of financial hardship

The previous chapter used people's opinions on the level of income required to make ends meet as a device for comparing poverty lines across geographical areas with different levels of income. The analysis now tries an alternative approach, based this time on measuring the actual impact of low incomes on a direct indicator of financially induced social exclusion.

Although the method used here will *not* make use of the standard indicators of 'deprivation', it is appropriate to discuss the theory behind the approach in terms of familiar analyses of the relationship between low income and low levels of consumption. There is a long history of such analysis in the UK (Townsend, 1979; Mack and Lansley, 1985; Gordon with others, 2000), and more recently in Ireland (Nolan and Whelan 1996). *Within* any country, a measure of household living standards is devised that takes account of as wide a range of items of consumption as possible. In the ECHP, for example, there are questions about the ownership of consumer durables and about the extent to which families can afford to keep their homes warm, entertain guests and so on. Still within the country, it can be shown that households with low levels of income report low scores on the composite index of living standards, and are said to be deprived.

There are two possible interpretations of the relationship between low income, deprivation and 'poverty'. One version says that deprivation, as a direct indicator of living standards and of social exclusion, *is* poverty, and that a low income is a potential *cause* of such poverty. That is the interpretation adopted by our Irish colleagues (Whelan with others, 2003). And it has been incorporated into the standard language of the European Union where households with incomes below 60% of their national median are no longer said to be 'in' poverty, but 'at risk of' poverty. The other version says that a low income *is* poverty, and that deprivation is a measure of the *consequences* of poverty. That is the interpretation implied by Townsend's seminal analyses (1979) of relative poverty.

It is not necessary to decide which of these interpretations is more appropriate, but we can take advantage of the second interpretation for our present purpose to propose a definition of an income poverty line as *a level of income below which the risk of exclusion exceeds a threshold value.*

Given the need to calibrate a set of poverty lines across countries and regions with very different overall living standards, the challenge is to find an indicator of exclusion that is not directly affected by overall living standards. The indicators of deprivation available from the ECHP are always calibrated separately within each country (Muffels and Fouarge, 2003; Whelan with others, 2001), because the consumption standards from which 'deprivation' is a deviation inevitably vary between countries. Most households in the Ile de France have a dishwasher. Very few in mainland Greece have one. Lack of a dishwasher would be seen as much more depriving in one place than the other. So deprivation scores have to be treated as relative to country, just as income is.

The ECHP does, however, contain two questions that may be interpreted as absolute rather than relative indicators of financial exclusion.

Considering your household's income as well as expenses: is there normally some money left which you could save?

Yes

No, or very little

Thinking of your household's total monthly income, is your household able to make ends meet ...

with great difficulty

with difficulty

with some difficulty

fairly easily

easily

very easily?

It can be argued that answers to these two questions would *not* be expected to vary systematically between places (or over time) as a direct consequence of variations in the average income against which citizens set their expectations. Households in all places (and at all times) will adjust their expenditure patterns and expectations to the social standards they see around them. Those with sufficient income to meet those standards will report that they are able to save and are managing well; those with insufficient income to meet those standards will report they are unable to save or to manage. If so, these two questions provide an opportunity to measure variations between countries, and between regions, in the social standards that are adopted.

The hypothesised relationships are shown in stylised form in Figure 8.a. A low-income area (for example, a country), a medium-income area and a high-

Figure 8.a: Stylised relationship between income, hardship and poverty

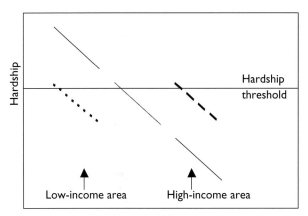

income area are assumed for illustrative purposes to have non-overlapping distributions of income. A measure of financial 'hardship' is designed to reflect households' inability to save and difficulty in managing, and is closely correlated with income in each area.

- If people in all three areas were influenced by a common set of social standards, then the relationships between income and hardship would be as illustrated by the three solid lines – in effect, one continuous line in which hardship is directly affected by income, irrespective of the average income of the area. In that case, all the people in the low-income area would have an income placing them above the hardship threshold, and would be poor; none of the people in the high-income area would be poor.

- If, on the other hand, people in each area were influenced by a set of social standards derived only from the conditions of the area in which they were living, then the relationships would be as illustrated for the low- and high-income areas by the dashed lines. The risk of hardship is determined solely by a household's position in the income distribution *relative to others in their own area*. The proportion of households whose income placed them above the hardship threshold, and were therefore poor, would be the same in each area.

These two relationships can both be expressed in terms of the following equation:

> Risk of hardship
> = α × household income
> + ß × area's average income
> + constant

In the first hypothesised model (the continuous solid line on the graph) the risk of hardship falls with income right across the range. The slope is given by α and will be negative. The area's average income has no effect on a household's risk of hardship, so ß will be zero. In the second hypothesised model (the dashed lines on the graph), the slope between households within each area (α) is the same as before, but areas with a high average income increase the risk of hardship for a household with any given income. The coefficient for the area effect (ß) will be positive. In the example given, where hardship is entirely determined by income relative to the average for the area, the area coefficient will be equal (and opposite) to the household effect.

So, if it assumed that the two questions contributing to the measure of hardship are not directly affected by the living standards of the area (country, region) in which people live, analysis of the point in the income distribution at which hardship passes a threshold in each area can be interpreted as a calibration of the area's poverty line. As in the previous chapter:

- if there is a strong tendency for households in richer *regions* to cross the hardship threshold at a higher income, that will favour the use of regionally defined poverty lines;
- if high-income *countries* are shown to have higher risks of hardship at each level of income, but there is little variation by region within countries, that will favour nationally defined thresholds; and
- if the relationship between income and hardship is constant across all regions and all countries, that will support the Europe-wide definition of poverty.

The index of hardship was derived by allocating between five and zero integer points for each of the six possible answers in the scale of responses to the question about how well households were managing, plus an additional two points if the householder reported that they were not able to save[15]. This provides a score of between zero and seven scale points.

As before, the clearest association between income and the hardship scale was found when the analysis used the householder's estimate of current income rather then the calculated sum of annual income (see page 9). The regression equation fitted best when income was expressed as a logarithm (which is much

---

[15] The scale was tested initially by regressing all six answers to the management question, and the savings question, as a series of dummy variables against log income. The metric of one point per scale position plus two for not saving came very close to replicating that equation, with the use of a single semi-continuous variable. Although strictly speaking an ordinal scale, the distribution of the hardship scores was approximately normal, and the area-by-area analysis used ordinary least squares techniques rather than ordered logit for ease of calculation.

more sensitive to variations at the lower than the upper end of the income distribution). If the regression equation *within each area* is written:

$$\text{hardship} = \alpha \times \text{Log}_n(\text{currinc}) + c$$

then the point at which income crosses the hardship threshold in that area can be calculated as:

$$\text{povline}_{hard} = \exp\frac{T\text{-}c}{\alpha}$$

where T is the chosen hardship threshold. The threshold chosen is arbitrary; a value of 3.3 was selected because it produced approximately the same number of households in 'poverty' across Europe as were counted using the conventional line based on 60% of the median. As before, it is not the level of the calculated 'hardship' poverty lines that matters for this analysis – it is the variation in those levels between areas with high and low average incomes.

As before, each country's hardship poverty line was calculated on the basis of a separate equation, in which both the slope (α) and the constant (c) were allowed to vary between countries. The estimates for regions within countries were based on the country-level equation, in which the slope was fixed for the country, while the constants were allowed to vary between regions.

Sweden has again been omitted because its survey does not include the hardship questions. The BHPS- and GSOEP-derived versions of the ECHP do not include the questions, so the British and German analysis has been based on the third (1996) wave of the original ECHP data instead of the sixth (1999) wave. Germany has again had to be omitted from the regional analysis, with the consequent loss of 12 units of analysis.

The risk-of-hardship poverty lines calculated for each country are plotted in Figure 8.b. In one sense, the findings are very similar to those for normative poverty lines. As before, there appears at first sight to be a negative relationship between national average incomes and the level at which a country's poverty line is pitched – that is, poorer countries appear to require a higher level of income to escape hardship – exactly the opposite of what relative poverty theory would lead us to predict. As before, it turns out that

Figure 8.b: Country-level hardship poverty lines, plotted against country median income

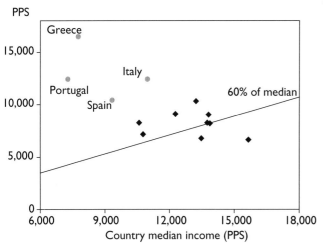

Note: Luxembourg's data (11,980 PPS = 52% of the median) are off the scale to the right. Sweden is omitted.

Figure 8.c: Region-level hardship poverty lines excluding southern Europe, plotted by regional median income

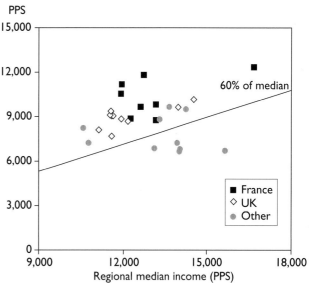

the countries in the top-left quadrant are the four southern countries. The extreme case this time is Greece, where the hardship analysis seems to place the poverty line at more than twice the national median. If we again make the risky assumption that there is something different about the way respondents in those countries perceived the questions about management and savings, the hardship poverty lines for the remaining countries are at more credible levels, around 60% of the median. But, unlike the analysis of normative poverty lines,

Table 8.1: Regression equations explaining country and regional hardship poverty lines in terms of country and regional median incomes: excluding southern Europe

	Analysis by country	**Analysis by region**
Median income of country	not significant	not significant
Median income of region	not applicable	0.27
Constant	11,492	5,547
Number of observations	10	28
R²	3.2%	7.2%

Note: A more technical version of the equations is provided in Table D3. For the regional analysis, an initial equation including the median incomes of each country and the deviation of regional incomes from the country median, were confined to countries with more than one region. The country-income coefficient was not significant; the equation actually shown included all countries, analysed absolute regional income and omitted country income.

the figure does *not* suggest any systematic relationship between hardship poverty lines and national median incomes among the remaining countries – far from being a constant proportion of the median, the slope of the implicit line linking the northern and continental countries appears flat. A simple regression equation linking median income with the hardship poverty line suggested that there was no significant slope (Table 8.1).

As before, we can also calculate a hardship poverty line for each region, and the results are plotted in Figure 8.c for the countries of northern and continental Europe – excluding the four southern countries. Within France, households in the Ile de France required a higher income to avoid hardship than those in other regions; within the UK, the prosperous regions of London and the South East also recorded higher poverty lines. The figure implies a general upward drift of poverty lines with higher regional incomes, although the slope calculated from a regression equation implies an increase of only 27 PPS in the poverty line for each 100 PPS increase in the median (Table 8.1). Crucially, however, the regression analysis confirms that the median income of the country had no effect – it was the regional average income that mattered.

Finally, Figure 8.d records the pattern of regional poverty lines in the four southern countries. There is no suggestion that the median income of the region has any effect on the level at which households fall into hardship.

Figure 8.d: Region-level hardship poverty lines in southern Europe, plotted by regional median income

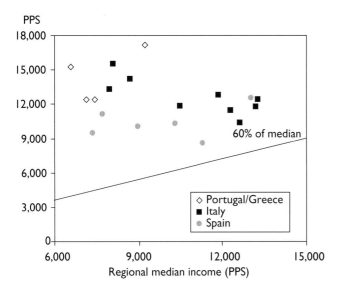

9

Where are Europe's poor?

The starting point for this study was the need for the European Union, and each of its member states, to know where poor households are located. In which countries is the poverty rate highest? In which regions within countries? These are questions that the EU itself needs answers to in its bid to 'take steps to make a decisive impact on the eradication of poverty'. Each member state needs answers to the same questions, partly because it is responsible to the Union for measures intended to eradicate poverty and partly because it will want to eradicate poverty for its own sake, independently of commonly agreed policy within the Union.

Income, inequality and poverty within countries

A substantial output from the analysis is a country-by-country and-region-by-region plot of the prevalence of poverty, which uses the standard conventional benchmark that defines the poor as households with an income below 60% of their country's median.

If we compare countries, it is striking that the range of within-country inequality is wider, and the rate of country-relative poverty higher, in countries that have low levels of national income measured in purchasing power standards (Tables 3.2 and 4.1; Figure 4.b). So, for example, the inequality index used for this research fell from as high as 0.25 in Portugal (whose median income is only 7,275 PPS per annum) to just 0.12 in Denmark (whose median income is as much as 15,658 PPS). As a result, the relative poverty rate using the conventional national benchmark fell from 23% in Portugal to 13% in

Denmark. The *persistent* poverty rate (defined as being below the poverty line for three consecutive years within a five-year period) fell from 20% in low-income Portugal to 3% in high-income Denmark (page 15). National relative poverty rates are higher in countries with low average incomes, not directly because of the low average incomes but because inequality is wider in those countries.

Many researchers have assumed that the most important influence on relative poverty rates would be the 'welfare regime' adopted in each country. If the countries of western Europe are allocated to four regimes ('social democratic', 'liberal', 'corporatist' and 'residual'), it appears that inequality is widest and poverty most prevalent in the liberal and residual states, and least prevalent in the social democratic ones (Tables 3.1 and 4.1; Figure 3.b). With only 15 units of observation and a strong association between potential explanatory variables, it is not possible to disentangle the effects very precisely. But if each country's welfare regime and median income are both plotted, then it looks as if the position of the country on the income scale is a more important influence than the welfare regime. On the other hand, analysis of the eastern *Länder* of Germany – the former DDR – suggests that a fifth welfare regime, 'ex-socialist', may be associated with less inequality and lower poverty rates than any of the four 'standard' regimes of western Europe (Figure 5.d). This point will be especially relevant to an analysis of the likely impact of the proposed enlargement of the Union, discussed below.

Another systematic difference between the more prosperous and the less prosperous European economies is in the range of inequalities at the top and the bottom of the scale (Figure 3.c). In low-income countries, disadvantaged households (represented by the lowest decile of the national income distribution) are even worse off than might otherwise have been expected; but this is rather a small effect. In the same low-income countries, privileged households (represented by the top decile of the national income distribution) are substantially better off than might otherwise have been expected. One consequence of this is that 'privileged' households in Portugal are much closer to their equivalents in Denmark; it is 'disadvantaged' households in Portugal whose purchasing power really suffers in comparison with their Danish counterparts (page 13). Another consequence of the variations in high inequality is that, if relative poverty is defined in relation to the top decile (rather than the median), then poverty rates in less prosperous counties such as Portugal are even higher, and the rates in more prosperous countries such as Denmark are even lower (Figure 4.b; Table 4.2).

All of the findings summarised so far suggest a very strong conclusion: that *relative* poverty is much more common in the countries of western Europe which have low average incomes – even though the average income has no direct effect on the measure of poverty. The association between poverty rates and national average incomes is probably understated by the most commonly used definition of poverty, namely, one year's income in relation to the median.

Income, inequality and poverty in regions

It was necessary to revise the standard regional classification so that all regions analysed were broadly similar in size. The income gap between the two regions of Greece is much wider than that between the regions of any of the other medium-sized countries (Figure 5.a). Among the five large countries, regional inequalities are widest in Italy and Spain, and least wide in Germany and the UK (Tables 5.2 and 5.3). The between-region inequality index is six times higher in Italy than in Germany.

The range of inequality *within* regions tends to be wider in countries with low overall average incomes (Figure 5.b). Three capital cities (Madrid, London and Paris) are notable for a combination of

exceptionally high incomes (relative to their country) and very high levels of inequality.

If poverty is defined relative to a regional benchmark, it is most common in south Portugal and least common in one or another of the east German regions (depending on the measure used, Table 6.1). If poverty is defined relative to a national benchmark (Figure 6.a), then both the highest and the lowest rates are to be found in the same country - Italy – because of the wide range of inequality between its regions. If all countries' and regions' poverty rates are measured relative to an EU-wide benchmark (Figure 6.b), then the prevalence ranges from 57% in mainland Greece, to 6% in Schleswig-Holstein and Hamburg, and down to 2% in Luxembourg (Table 4.2). That range is worth repeating: more than half of mainland Greeks are in Euro-poverty; only one in 50 of the Luxembourgeois.

Relative to where: regional, national or EU-wide benchmarks?

One of the unexpected findings of the analysis was that relative poverty is more common in the less prosperous countries of Europe even if national benchmarks are applied. But the finding that the 'poorest' countries and regions have more 'poor' households if poverty is measured against an EU-wide benchmark was entirely predictable. How can we decide on the most appropriate basis for defining 'relative poverty'? Although Eurostat provides estimates of poverty in relation to European as well as national benchmarks, the official position, confirmed by the Laeken summit, is that national relativities are most appropriate. Most analysts have followed suit. Plausible cases can be made either to shrink or to expand the geographical frame of reference.

- If poverty is relative, should it not be defined in relation to the distribution of income in the immediate region where people live? And would that not provide greater consistency of treatment between small countries (with one or two regions) and large countries (with 10 or 12)?
- If the European Union is a geographical, political, economic and increasingly social entity, should the definition of poverty not be defined in terms of

the goods and services that people can (or cannot) buy, irrespective of where in the Union they live?

Although statistical analysis can illustrate the effects of choosing alternative spatial frameworks for the definition of poverty, it does not necessarily show which is the most appropriate (page 5). The answer may depend on largely political issues, according to people's and politicians' sense of the geographical and administrative unit which most closely expresses their sense of identity. Alternatively, it can be argued that the boundaries of the community with which households are compared should coincide with the administrative unit with the primary responsibility for the relevant set of policies. Both the political and the administrative criteria probably point to national benchmarks, although even that conclusion may vary between countries.

A third approach is to find out how far people's perception of 'social exclusion' is influenced by their perception of the standard of living they see around them within their own region or in their own country; or whether they feel equally excluded (on a given income) wherever they live. The ECHP has provided an opportunity to test this approach, using two measures of households' sense of exclusion to calibrate poverty lines. If people living in better-off *regions* tended to think more money (purchasing power) was needed to make ends meet than those living in worse-off regions, that would favour the use of poverty lines related to regional benchmarks. If high-income *countries* expressed higher expectations than low-income countries (but there was little difference between regions within countries), that would favour national benchmarks. But if the amount of purchasing power required to make ends meet were similar, whatever the overall position of the region and the country, that would favour a single EU-wide benchmark.

Both of the experimental approaches outlined in Chapters 7 and 8 showed that the poverty lines indicated in the four southern countries (Portugal, Spain, Italy and Greece) were unrealistically high (Figures 7.b and 8.b). Almost everyone in those countries felt that they were unable to make ends meet! We can make sense of the analysis only if these four countries are omitted – but such a selective approach raises *very* severe doubts about the reliability

of the remainder of the interpretation. Among the other 11 countries:

- one of the two experimental analyses suggests that the income of the region has an important effect on perceptions of exclusion; but the income of the country has no effect, after account is taken of the regional position (Table 7.1);
- the other experimental analysis suggests that the income of the region has a smaller effect; but there is still no influence attributable to the income of the country (Table 8.1).

It can be argued, on this basis, that poverty lines should be a compromise between a regional and an EU-wide standard, with no direct reference to the country. Perhaps it could use the formula proposed by Atkinson for pooling country and EU perspectives (see page 4), but with the regional median substituted for the national median.

It should be remembered, however, that the political and administrative perspectives just outlined probably favour the use of national benchmarks. The research has cast doubt on the current almost-universal assumption that national benchmarks are most appropriate; but it does not provide conclusive arguments in favour of any of the three standards: regional, national or Europe-wide.

To the extent that poverty benchmarks placed more weight on regional than national relativities, the effects would be most striking in those countries with the widest gaps between regions: Greece, Italy and Spain (Figure 5.a; Table 5.2). Using regional benchmarks would reduce the apparent number of poor households in mainland Greece, in Sicily and Sardinia, and in central Spain (excluding Madrid); it would increase the apparent number of poor households in Attica and the Greek islands, in Lombardy and in Madrid itself. Perhaps the debate about regional standards should take place in these countries with wide regional disparities rather than in the remainder of countries less affected by the issue. Ironically, these three are among the four countries whose results from the empirical calibration experiments had to be rejected as inconsistent with our hypotheses. So the evidence in favour of within-region comparisons is derived from the northern European countries least likely to be affected.

To the extent that poverty benchmarks placed more weight on EU-wide than national relativities, the effects would be most striking in the countries at either end of the prosperity scale (Table 3.1; Figure 5.b). The number of poor households would appear to rise in Portugal and Greece while they fell in Luxembourg and Denmark. A change in definition along those lines would have major political implications for the Union. National benchmarks minimise the apparent variations in poverty rates between member states, and encourage national governments to retain responsibility for anti-poverty policies. Cross-national benchmarks would reveal wider variations between states, would call for more transfers of resources between countries, and would assign greater responsibility for policy to EU institutions. Research contributes to, but does not answer, these essentially political questions.

Expanding the Union

All this analysis is based on the European Union at its current (2003) boundaries. Ten more countries are to 'accede' to the EU in 2004, and a further three are 'candidates' to join at some later stage. The current research has not directly studied the distributions of income in the candidate countries. But it worth considering what the implications of the current analysis might be for the new Europe.

Most of the candidate countries have lower levels of overall prosperity than most of the existing member states, whether this is measured conventionally by the national accounts (Eurostat, 2003) or in terms of the median income used for in this study (Dennis and Guio, 2003b). Only three of the acceding countries (Cyprus, Slovenia and Malta) have incomes within the range covered by the existing membership. The other acceding and candidate countries have incomes well below those experienced in the current Union, down to Romania, whose median is as low as 10% of the Danish figure.

The four acceding countries that were not members of the Soviet bloc (Turkey, Slovenia, Malta and Cyprus) have national relative poverty rates that are not inconsistent with the patterns observed among existing member states, in which countries with low median incomes have high poverty rates (Figure 9.a). Turkey is the outstanding case, with the highest

poverty rate and the second-lowest median income of all the countries studied.

On the other hand, the ex-socialist countries, all with low median incomes, have lower poverty rates than might have been expected from the relationship found in the western economies. These findings are consistent with the idea, initially based on the East German regions, that 'ex-socialist' regimes are still less unequal than other countries (Flemming and Micklewright, 2000).

If Turkey eventually joins the Union, it can be expected to make a substantial contribution to the number of European households that are defined as poor against national benchmarks; but the transition countries will import proportionately fewer relatively poor households. If poverty were defined against a single EU-wide benchmark, however, a very different picture would emerge. The number of poor households in the 'old' Union would fall (because the benchmark would be adjusted downwards), while a very large proportion of households in the accession and candidate countries would be seen to be poor.

Figure 9.a: National relative poverty rates, EU members compared with accession and candidate countries

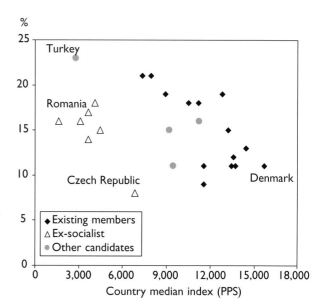

Source: Dennis and Guio (2003a, 2003b). Hungary and the Slovak Republic are not covered. The black diamonds representing the current EU member states are equivalent to those in Figure 4.a, although there are some slight differences between the two versions.

Wider, and narrower, perspectives

This analysis has considered the distribution of household income from an EU perspective. It is from that position that it is relevant to ask what spatial framework should define relative poverty – whether the national benchmarks currently used should be replaced with a narrower reference group (the region) or a wider reference group (the Union). The study has shown that the choice is an important one, although it stops short of saying which reference point should be adopted.

One argument may be that applying a common poverty line across national boundaries is a fundamental breach of the Townsend (1979) principle of relativity. The fundamentalist interpretation of that principle is that a family may be poor in Denmark because it is excluded from the way of life of that country, even though the purchasing power of that family would make it quite well off in Portugal. The possibility of extending that comparison to Turkey illustrates the point rather vividly[16]. That view tends to support the continued use of national benchmarks or even a move to regional ones.

The argument for a common European benchmark does not rest, however, on a reinterpretation of poverty to mean absolute rather than relative deprivation. The argument is that, as the peoples of the Union become more closely knit within a single community, they will naturally develop a common perception of a way of life that may apply consistently from Dublin and Lisbon to Berlin and Athens – and may eventually extend to Vilnius and to Ankara. Poverty would still be relative even if the reference group were extended. A distinct, but parallel, argument is that, as the governments of the Union become more closely integrated in the development of the Union's social policy, EU institutions will be expected to address inequalities between nations while domestic governments retain responsibility for inequalities within nations.

If the benchmark were to extend wider, to the 15-member EU, and then wider still to the prospective 28-member EU, what logic stops the argument there? Why not a common benchmark covering the whole geographical continent of Europe? Indeed, why not a common poverty line covering the whole world? In fact, Milanovic (2002) has addressed precisely that issue, showing that the number of European households that would be counted as poor would be very small indeed if the poverty line were defined as 60% of the world median income. Most of the world's poor are in Africa and Asia.

The answer to this question of perspective may be an institutional one. Policy makers could adopt a framework appropriate to the scale of the issues under consideration.

- To the extent that some regional governments (for example, in Germany and parts of the UK) have powers that affect the distribution of income, then a regional benchmark may be appropriate to them.
- When considering their own domestic responsibilities, national governments could apply a national benchmark.
- EU institutions, and national governments when addressing European issues, could consider the distribution of income across the Union, and measure poverty against a common benchmark. Between-country inequalities could be seen as a European issue, even if within-country inequalities remained the responsibility of national governments.
- The United Nations and other global institutions could indeed look at the whole world, and define poverty in terms of a single standard. So could national governments when contributing to UN debates or considering their own worldwide development policies.

---

[16] The lowest decile in Denmark (8,495 PPS) is actually higher than the median in Portugal (7,275 PPS) (see Table 3.1 and page 13). It is probably about the level of the top decile in Turkey.

References

Atkinson, A. (1995) 'Income distribution in Europe and the United States', *Oxford Review of Economic Policy*, vol 12, no 1.

Atkinson, A. (1998) *Poverty in Europe*, Oxford: Basil Blackwell.

Atkinson, A. (2003) 'Income inequality in OECD countries: data and explanations' (CESifo Working Paper 881), Munich: Center for Economic Studies and Ifo Institute for Economic Research.

Atkinson, A. and Bourguignon, F. (2000) *Handbook of income distribution*, Amsterdam: Elsevier.

Atkinson, A., Cantillon, B., Marlier, E. and Nolan, B. (2002) *Social indicators: The EU and social inclusion*, Oxford: Oxford University Press.

Atkinson, A., Gardiner, K., Lechêne, V. and Sutherland, H. (1998) 'Comparing poverty rates across countries: a case study of France and the United Kingdom', in S. Jenkins, A. Kapteyn and M. van Praag, M. (eds) *The distribution of welfare and household production: International perspectives*, Cambridge: Cambridge University Press.

Atkinson, A., Rainwater, L. and Smeeding, T. (1995) *Income distribution in OECD countries*, Paris: OECD.

Beblo, M. and Knau, T. (2001) 'Measuring income inequality in Euroland', *Review of Income and Wealth*, vol 47, no 3.

Berthoud, R. (2001) 'Rich place, poor place: area variations in household income within Britain', ISER Working Paper 2001-2, Colchester: University of Essesx

Berthoud, R. and Ford, R. (1996) *Relative needs: Variations in the living standards of different types of household*, London: Policy Studies Institute.

Berthoud, R. and Iacovou, M. (eds) (2004) *Social Europe: Living standards and welfare states*, Cheltenham: Edward Elgar.

Blackburn, M. (1998) 'The sensitivity of international poverty comparisons', *Review of Income and Wealth*, vol 44, no 4.

Cowell, F.A. (1995) *Measuring inequality*, London: Prentice-Hall/Harvester-Wheatsheaf.

Deleeck, H., van den Bosch, K. and de Lathouwer, L. (1992) *Poverty and the adequacy of social security in the EC*, Aldershot: Avebury.

Dennis, I. and Guio, A. (2003a) 'Poverty and social exclusion in the EU after Laeken – part 1', *Statistics in Focus 8/2003*, Luxembourg: Eurostat.

Dennis, I. and Guio, A. (2003b) 'Monetary poverty in EU acceding and candidate countries', *Statistics in Focus 21/2003*, Luxembourg: Eurostat.

Esping-Andersen, G. (1990) *The three worlds of welfare capitalism*, Cambridge: Polity Press.

Esping-Andersen, G. (1999) *Social foundations of past industrial economies*, Oxford: Oxford University Press.

Eurostat (2003) *Eurostat Yearbook 2003*, Luxembourg: Commission of the European Communities.

Ferarra, M. (1996) 'The "southern model" of welfare in social Europe', *Journal of European Social Policy*, vol 6, no 1.

Flemming, J. and Micklewright, J. (2000) 'Income distribution, economic systems and transition', in A. Atkinson and F. Bourguignon (eds) *Handbook of income distribution*, Amsterdam: Elsevier.

Gordon, D. (2000) 'Measuring absolute and overall poverty', in D. Gordon. and P. Townsend *Breadline Europe: The measurement of poverty*, Bristol: The Policy Press, pp 49-77.

Gordon, D., Adelman, L., Ashworth, K., Bradshaw, J., Levitas, R., Middleton, S., Pantazis, C., Patsios, D., Payne, S., Townsend, P. and Williams, J. (2000) *Poverty and social exclusion in Britain*, York: Joseph Rowntree Foundation.

Gordon, D. and Townsend, P. (2000) *Breadline Europe: The measurement of poverty*, Bristol: The Policy Press.

Gottschalk, P. and Smeeding, T. (2000) 'Empirical evidence on income inequality in industrialised countries', in A. Atkinson and F. Bourguignon (eds) *Handbook of income distribution*, Amsterdam: Elsevier.

Hagenaars, A. (1986) *The perception of poverty*, Amsterdam: North Holland.

Hagenaars, A., de Vos, K. and Zaid, A. (1998) 'Patterns of poverty in Europe', in S. Jenkins, A. Kapteyn and M. van Praag (eds) *The distribution of welfare and household production: International perspectives*, Cambridge: Cambridge University Press.

Jargowsky, P. (1996) *Poverty and place: Ghettos, barrios and the American city*, New York, NY: Russell Sage.

Jenkins, S. (1991) 'The measurement of income inequality', in L. Osberg (ed) *Economic inequality and poverty: International perspectives*, Armonk, NY: Sharpe.

Jenkins, S. (1999) 'sg104 Analysis of income distributions (sumdist, xfrac, ineqdeco, inecdec0, geivars, ineqfac, povdeco)', *Stata Technical Bulletin* STB-48.

Jesuit, D., Rainwater, L. and Smeeding, T. (2003) 'Regional poverty in the rich countries', in Y. Amiel and J. Bishop (eds) 'Inequality, welfare and poverty: theory and measurement', *Research on Economic Inequality: A Research Annual*, vol 9.

Johnston, R., Gregory, D. and Smith, D. (1994) *Dictionary of human geography*, Oxford: Basil Blackwell.

Kangas, O. and Ritakallio, V. (2002) 'Relative to what? Cross-national picture of European poverty measured by regional, national and European standards', Unpublished paper presented at EU COST A15 meeting, 6 April.

Mack, J. and Lansley, S. (1985) *Poor Britain*, London: Allen and Unwin

Milanovic, B. (2002) 'True world income distribution, 1988 and 1993: first calculations based on household surveys alone', *Economic Journal*.

Muffels, R. and Fouarge, D. (2003) *The role of European welfare states in explaining resources deprivation*, EPAG Working Paper 41, University of Essex.

Nolan, B. and Whelan, C. (1996) *Resources, deprivation and poverty*, Oxford: Clarendon Press.

Nolan, B., Whelan, C. and Williams, J. (1998) *Where are poor households? The spatial distribution of poverty and deprivation in Ireland*, Dublin: Combat Poverty Agency.

Openshaw, S. (1977) 'A geographical study of scale and aggregation problems in region-building, partitioning and spatial modelling', *Transactions of the Institute of British Geographers*, vol 2, no 1.

Popova, M. (1996) *Income inequality and poverty of economies in transition*, Working Paper 144, Luxembourg: Luxembourg Income Study.

Rainwater, L., Smeeding, T. and Coder, J. (1999) *Poverty across states, nations and continents*, Luxembourg: Luxembourg Income Study.

Ringen, S. (1991) 'Households, standard of living and inequality', *Review of Income and Wealth*, vol 37.

Runciman, W. (1966) *Relative deprivation and social justice*, London: Routledge and Kegan Paul.

Smeeding, T. (2000) 'American income inequality in a cross-national perspective: why are we so different?', in K. Vleminckx and T. Smeeding (eds) *Child well-being, child poverty and child policy in modern nations*, Bristol: The Policy Press.

Smeeding, T., O'Higgins, M. and Rainwater, M. (eds) (1990) *Poverty, inequality and income distribution in comparative perspective*, Hemel Hempstead: Harvester Wheatsheaf.

Szulc, A. (1996) *Economic transition and poverty: the case of the Visegrad countries*, Working Paper 138, Luxembourg: Luxembourg Income Study.

Townsend, P. (1979) *Poverty in the United Kingdom*, Harmondsworth: Penguin.

Whelan, C., Layte, R., Maître, B. and Nolan, B. (2001) 'Income, deprivation and economic strain', *European Sociological Review*, vol 17, no 4.

Whelan, C., Layte, R., Maître, B. and Nolan, B. (2003) 'Persistent income poverty and deprivation in the European Union', *Journal of Social Policy*, vol 32, no 2.

Wirtz, C. and Mejer, L. (2002) 'The European Community Household Panel (ECHP)', *Journal of Applied Social Science Studies (Schmollers Jahrbuch)*, vol 122, no 1.

Appendix A:
Glossary of technical terms and abbreviations

Annual income	In the ECHP, annual income is defined as the total income of the household's current members during the calendar year prior to the date of interview, as calculated by Eurostat on the basis of detailed questions about each income source. See also current income.
BHPS	British Household Panel Survey
Current income	In the ECHP, current income is defined as the total normal income of the household at the time of the interview, as estimated by the household respondent (expressed here at an annual rate). See also annual income.
Decile	See percentile
ECHP	European Community Household Panel survey; see Chapter 2
EPAG	European Panel Analysis Group
Equivalent income	Household income divided by a factor reflecting the number and ages of household members to provide an indication of income in relation to needs. The equivalence scale used in this analysis was the modified OECD scale: 1.0 for the first adult, plus 0.5 for each additional adult, plus 0.3 for each child.
EU	European Union
Europe	The word 'Europe' is almost always used here to refer to the EU and its 15 member states in 1999 rather than to the continent as a whole.
GDP	Gross Domestic Product – the total economic output of a country, as estimated by the national accounts.
GSOEP	German Socio-Economic Panel
Inequality index	The measure of inequality between households, between regions and between countries used in this analysis. See pages 9-10 of text
ISER	Institute for Social and Economic Research, University of Essex
Logarithm (log)	A function (of income) that is more sensitive to variations between low values, and less sensitive to variations between high values, than the standard metric.
Mean	The average income calculated by dividing the sum of all incomes by the total number of households. See also median.
Mean logarithmic deviation	See inequality index, and pages 9-10 of text
Median	See percentile
Net income	Household income including social security benefits but after subtracting taxes.
NUTS	Nomenclature of Territorial Units for Statistics – that is, regions and sub-regions.
Percentile	If a representative group of 1,000 households were placed in order from lowest to highest incomes, the first percentile represents the income of the 10th (lowest), the tenth percentile the income of the 100th and so on up to the 99th percentile representing the 990th (highest). The tenth percentile is also known as the lowest decile, while the 90th percentile is the highest decile. The 50th percentile (the middle income in the range) is known as the median.

PPS	Purchasing power standards; the unit of account for measuring incomes across countries; see page 9.
R^2	(Pronounced R squared.) A measure of how accurately a regression equation predicts the outcome for all members of the sample. It can be interpreted as indicating the proportion of variance explained by the equation.
Region	Always used here to refer to subdivisions of countries rather than to groups of countries. See pages 17-18 and Appendix C for definitions of the 'regions' used in this analysis.
Regression equation	An analytical technique that calculates a formula which most closely explains the relationship between a 'dependent' variable and one or more explanatory variables.
Weighting	Data for each household are weighted by two factors to ensure that the analysis is representative of the population of each country and of Europe. See page 8.

Appendix B: Comparing 'annual' with 'current' income

The ECHP provides two measures of each household's income.

- One, referred to here as 'current income', is based on asking the householder to provide a single figure for the aggregate income of the whole household during the current week or month.
- The other, referred to here as 'annual income', is based on detailed questions asking each member of the household to report the amount of each source of income (earnings, dividends, pensions, social security benefits and so on) received during each month of the calendar year prior to the interview (thus, 1998 for the 1999 survey).

As discussed in Chapter 2, there are advantages and disadvantages of each measure. The annual income measure was used to calculate inequality indices and poverty rates in Chapters 3 to 6, to maximise consistency with other analyses. The current income measure was used to calibrate poverty lines in Chapters 7 and 8 because it was more closely associated with the dependent variables used in the calibration experiments. Remember that all data refer to 1999 except for UK (ECHP), Luxembourg, and Germany (ECHP), where 1996 data were used, and inflated to 1999 prices.

Tables B.1 and B.2 provide some simple comparisons. Table B.1 shows the extent to which the two

Table B.1: Differences between current and annual measures of income

	Correlation between current and annual	Median income			Inequality index		
		Current	Annual	A>C	Current	Annual	A>C
Finland	0.74	**9,367**	**10,782**	+15%	0.139	0.169	+22%
Denmark	0.59	14,601	15,658	+7%	0.120	0.115	−4%
UK (BHPS)	0.69	12,538	12,287	−2%	0.207	0.209	+1%
UK (ECHP)	0.72	13,251	13,920	+5%	0.190	0.203	+7%
Ireland	0.58	9,587	10,593	+10%	0.169	0.210	+24%
Netherlands	0.54	12,216	13,464	+10%	**0.087**	**0.141**	**+63%**
Belgium	**0.47**	**12,321**	**13,878**	+13%	**0.092**	**0.181**	**+96%**
Luxembourg	0.84	21,696	22,816	+5%	0.122	0.147	+20%
France	**0.29**	12,752	13,223	+4%	0.230	0.164	−29%
Germany (SOEP)	0.71	12,880	13,757	+7%	0.122	0.142	+17%
Germany (ECHP)	0.71	13,321	14,298	+7%	0.100	0.158	+58%
Austria	0.74	12,832	13,815	+8%	0.105	0.162	+55%
Portugal	0.85	6,896	7,275	+6%	0.228	0.254	+12%
Spain	0.88	9,678	9,352	−3%	0.179	0.208	+16%
Italy	0.78	10,141	10,975	+8%	0.144	0.173	+20%
Greece	0.65	7,507	7,766	+3%	0.234	0.235	+1%

Note: Sweden has been omitted as it does not provide a current income measure.

measures differ, country by country. These statistics do not show which of the two is better; but, where they provide widely divergent conclusions, one should treat both sources with some caution. In each panel of the table, the two data sets with the widest divergence are highlighted in bold print.

The first panel of Table B.1 uses a correlation coefficient to show how far households with high or low incomes in each country on one measure were similarly high or low on the other. The consistency between the two was impressively high in Spain, Portugal and Luxembourg, but worryingly low in Belgium, and especially in France.

In most countries, median annual income was rather higher than median current income. This is not what would have been expected given that the current income was reported a few months later. The gap was widest in Finland and Belgium.

In some countries, such as Denmark, the UK and Greece, the measure of income inequality was almost identical whichever income definition was used. In many countries (with the notable exception of France), the annual income measure indicated wider inequality than the current income measure – contrary to expectation, because the annual measure, smoothed over a longer period, should show narrower inequality. The inequality measures in the Netherlands, and especially in Belgium, are highly sensitive to the definition of income.

Table B.2 offers two further comparisons. On both of the new calculations, a high correlation should encourage confidence in the validity of the income measure, so it is possible to say which income definition seems to be 'better' on each criterion. This time the lowest absolute correlations in each column are highlighted (rather than the biggest differences between income measures).

The first panel shows the extent to which households with high or low (log) incomes also reported low or high scores on a deprivation index. In every country, current income was more closely associated with a standard of living measure than was annual income. In Denmark, both income measures were weakly associated with deprivation, and this may suggest a genuinely weak link in that country. In Belgium, the correlation between annual income and deprivation was worryingly weak.

The second panel of Table B.2 calculates how far households with high or low incomes 'this year' had similarly high or low incomes 'last year', for those households that the ECHP records to have continued in roughly the same structure from one year to the next (that is, retained the same household identity number). In some countries, annual income appears to be more reliable on this diagnostic; in other countries, it seems less reliable. Current income was worryingly inconsistent between years in the UK ECHP and in France.

Table B.2: Consistency of current and annual measures of income

	Correlation with deprivation index			Correlation with previous year		
	Current	**Annual**	**A>C**	**Current**	**Annual**	**A>C**
Finland	−0.53	−0.45	+22%	0.66	0.72	+9%
Denmark	**−0.40**	**−0.32**	−4%	0.62	0.78	+27%
UK (BHPS)	na	na	na	0.60	0.81	+35%
UK (ECHP)	−0.59	−0.44	+7%	**0.39**	0.76	**+94%**
Ireland	−0.46	−0.41	+24%	0.73	0.75	+2%
Netherlands	−0.50	−0.43	**+63%**	0.76	**0.54**	−29%
Belgium	−0.47	**−0.34**	**+96%**	0.82	**0.61**	−26%
Luxembourg	−0.53	−0.48	+20%	0.83	0.84	+2%
France	−0.52	−0.47	−29%	**0.24**	0.79	**+223%**
Germany (SOEP)	na	na	+17%	0.79	0.78	−1%
Germany (ECHP)	−0.57	−0.41	+58%	0.80	0.76	−5%
Austria	−0.46	−0.42	+55%	0.85	0.73	−14%
Portugal	−0.65	−0.57	+12%	0.88	0.88	0%
Spain	−0.58	−0.47	16%	0.79	0.80	1%
Italy	−0.57	−0.53	20%	0.76	0.82	7%
Greece	−0.62	−0.56	1%	0.64	0.71	11%

Note: Sweden has been omitted as it did not provide a current income measure.

Appendix C:
Grouping regions

Table C.1 shows the complete list of NUTS1 regions as coded in the ECHP data, with an estimate of the number of households in each region, in thousands. The estimate was derived from grossing up the weighted survey data to known national totals, not by consulting populations statistics for each region.

As discussed in Chapter 5, small regions were grouped together so that as far as possible all regions had broadly the same number of households. The boxes in the table show which regions were grouped together, and the last two columns show the name

given to the group and its total number of households.

Regions are named in the first column of this table in national languages and spellings. The substantive tables and figures in Chapters 5 and 6 and Appendix D translate compass points into English, and apply English names where these are in common use (for example, Bayern becomes Bavaria, Méditeranée becomes Mediterranean, but Ile de France remains in French as it is never known as French Island!

Table C.1: Regions and grouped regions

Country	NUTS1 Region	Estimated number of households (000s)	Grouped region	Estimated number of households (000s)
Finland	Uusimaa	650		
	Etelä-Suomi (incl Åland)	870		
	Itä-Suomi	310		
	Väli-Suomi	300		
	Pohjois-Suomi	230	Finland	2,360
Sweden	Stockholm	810		
	Ostra mellansverige	800		
	Smaland med Oarna	630	Stockholm and South East	2,240
	Syssverige	460		
	Vastsverige	230		
	Norra mellasverige	280		
	Mellersta norrland	410		
	Ovra norrland	920	Rest of Sweden	2,300
Denmark		2,430	Denmark	2,430

continued.../

Table C.1: contd.../

Country	NUTS1 Region	Estimated number of households (000s)	Grouped region	Estimated number of households (000s)
UK	North	1,090	North	1,090
	Yorkshire and Humberside	1,920	Yorkshire and Humberside	1,920
	East Midlands	1,840		
	East Anglia	870	East Midlands/East Anglia	2,710
	London	3,590	London	3,590
	South East	3,700	South East	3,700
	South West	1,860	South West	1,860
	West Midlands	2,120	West Midlands	2,120
	North West	2,610	North West	2,610
	Wales	1,220		
	Northern Ireland	590	Wales/Northern Ireland	1,810
	Scotland	2,110	Scotland	2,110
Ireland	Ireland, excluding Dublin	880		
	Dublin	380	Ireland	1,260
Netherlands	Noord	570		
	Oost	2,660	North/East	3,230
	West	2,390	West	2,390
	Zuid	1,130	South	1,130
Belgium	Vlaams Gewest	2,370	Flanders	2,370
	Région Wallonne	1,380		
	Brussels	470	Walloon/Brussels	1,850
Luxembourg		160		
France	Ile de France	4,480	Ile de France	4,480
	Bassin Parisien	4,190	Bassin Parisien	4,190
	Nord – Pas-de-Calais	1,510	North – Pas-de-Calais	1,510
	Est	2,030	East	2,030
	Ouest	3,170	West	3,170
	Sud-Ouest	2,570	South Eest	2,570
	Centre-Est	2,830	Central-East	2,830
	Méditerranée	3,040	Mediterranean	3,040
Germany	Baden Württemberg	4,600	Baden Wurttemberg	4,600
	Bayern	5,250	Bavaria	5,250
	Berlin	1,780	Berlin	1,780
	Brandenburg	1,130	Brandenburg/Mecklenburg	1,940
	Mecklenburg-Vorpommern	810	-West Pomerania	
	Hessen	2,700	Hesse	2,700
	Niedersachsen	3,500		
	Bremen	350	Lower Saxony/Bremen	3,850
	Nordrhein-Westfallen	8,190	North Rhine-Westphalia	8,190
	Rheinland-Pfalz Saarland*	2,230	Rhineland-Palatinate/Saarland	2,230
	Sachsen	2,100	Saxony	2,100
	Sachsen-Anhalt	1,210	Saxony-Anhalt	1,210
	Schleswig Holstein	1,280	Schleswig Holstein/Hamburg	2,200
	Hamburg	920		
	Thüringen	1,070	Thuringia	1,070
Austria	Ostösterreich	1,470	East	1,470
	Südösterreich	670		
	Westösterreich	1,100	South/West	1,770

continued.../

Table C.1: contd.../

Country	NUTS1 Region	Estimated number of households (000s)	Grouped region	Estimated number of households (000s)
Portugal	Norte	540		
	Centro	730		
	Lisboa e Vale do Tejo	430	North/Central/Lisbon	1,700
	Alentejo	360		
	Algarve	430		
	Açores	390		
	Madeira	410	South and islands	1,590
Spain	Noroeste	1,370	North West	1,370
	Noreste	1,380	North East	1,380
	Comunidad de Madrid	1,620	Madrid	1,620
	Centro	1,760	Centre	1,760
	Este	3,780	East	3,780
	Sur	2,480		
	Canarias	470	South and Canaries	2,950
Italy	Nord Ovest	2,610	North West	2,610
	Lombardia	3,560	Lombardy	3,560
	Nord Est	2,490	North East	2,490
	Emilia-Romagna	1,610	Emilia-Romagna	1,610
	Centro	2,220	Centre	2,220
	Lazio	2,090	Lazio	2,090
	Abruzzo-Molise	590		
	Campania	1,920	Abruzzo-Molise/Campania	2,510
	Sud	2,220	South	2,220
	Sicilia	1,780		
	Sardegna	550	Islands	2,330
Greece	Voreia Ellada	1,190		
	Kentriki Ellada	770	Mainland Greece	1,960
	Attiki	1,520		
	Nisia Aigaiou, Kriti	360	Attica and islands	1,880

Note: *Already merged in the data file.

Appendix D:
Selected income statistics by country and by region

Table D.1: Selected income statistics by country

Country	Sample size	Median income (PPS)		Inequality index (mean log dev)		Poverty rate (national benchmark)	
		Median	Standard error	Index	Standard error	%	Standard error
Finland	3,822	10,782	102	0.169	0.007	16.0	0.7
Sweden	5,165	10,724	71	0.126	0.006	10.8	0.5
Denmark	2,387	15,658	155	0.115	0.007	13.3	0.7
UK	4,951	12,287	135	0.209	0.008	19.4	0.6
Ireland	2,378	10,593	175	0.210	0.018	22.7	0.9
Netherlands	5,023	13,464	131	0.141	0.006	10.9	0.5
Belgium	2,712	13,878	156	0.181	0.020	14.1	0.7
Luxembourg	933	22,816	465	0.147	0.012	12.2	1.1
France	5,610	13,223	105	0.164	0.009	16.1	0.5
Germany	5,847	13,757	103	0.142	0.006	13.4	0.5
Austria	2,815	13,815	164	0.162	0.008	15.4	0.7
Portugal	4,683	7,275	91	0.254	0.008	22.8	0.6
Spain	5,418	9,352	107	0.208	0.007	17.8	0.5
Italy	6,370	10,975	111	0.173	0.005	17.7	0.5
Greece	3,986	7,766	102	0.235	0.008	21.1	0.6

Notes: All calculations based on weighted data, using the Stata analysis program.

The median and its standard error calculated using *quantile regression.*

The inequality index (mean logarithmic deviation) and its standard error calculated using *svygei3*, written by Stephen P. Jenkins.

The poverty rate and its standard error calculated using *svymean.*

Table D.2: Selected income statistics by region

Country	Region	Sample size	Median income (PPS) Median	Median income (PPS) Standard error	Inequality index (mean log dev) Index	Inequality index (mean log dev) Standard error	Poverty rate (national benchmark) %	Poverty rate (national benchmark) Standard error
Finland	Finland	3,822	10,782	102	0.169	0.007	16.0	0.7
Sweden	Stockholm and South East	2,556	11,067	156	0.142	0.010	10.5	0.7
	Rest of Sweden	2,609	10,417	103	0.106	0.007	11.0	0.7
Denmark	Denmark	2,387	15,658	155	0.115	0.007	13.3	0.7
UK	North England	302	11,584	494	0.175	0.021	22.4	2.5
	Yorkshire and Humberside	477	11,121	327	0.172	0.015	22.0	2.0
	East Midlands/East Anglia	654	11,586	289	0.198	0.022	22.8	1.7
	South East England	780	13,962	345	0.211	0.021	13.6	1.3
	London	606	14,530	478	0.258	0.034	14.5	1.5
	South West England	450	11,639	421	0.188	0.018	20.1	2.0
	West Midlands	433	11,526	406	0.191	0.017	22.0	2.1
	North West England	519	11,921	386	0.202	0.016	21.2	1.9
	Wales/Northern Ireland	273	11,548	505	0.194	0.025	23.1	2.6
	Scotland	457	12,162	427	0.181	0.020	20.5	2.0
Ireland	Ireland	2,378	10,593	175	0.210	0.018	22.7	0.9
Netherlands	North/East	2,423	13,121	139	0.143	0.008	12.9	0.7
	West	1,758	14,016	239	0.141	0.012	8.8	0.7
	South	842	14,060	352	0.133	0.013	9.4	1.1
Belgium	Brussels/Walloon	1,602	13,649	237	0.164	0.014	13.7	0.9
	Flanders	1,110	13,948	196	0.194	0.033	14.3	1.1

continued

Table D.2: contd.../

Country	Region	Sample size	Median income (PPS)		Inequality index (mean log dev)		Poverty rate (national benchmark)	
			Median	Standard error	Index	Standard error	%	Standard error
France	Ile de France	847	16,694	350	0.209	0.030	11.2	1.1
	Bassin Parisien	1,033	12,639	271	0.175	0.024	17.4	1.2
	North – Pas-de-Calais	365	11,920	409	0.134	0.014	19.6	2.0
	East	525	13,165	312	0.106	0.009	14.6	1.5
	West	871	12,275	263	0.134	0.010	19.8	1.4
	South West	662	11,956	277	0.141	0.009	19.9	1.5
	Central East	633	13,155	287	0.148	0.015	15.9	1.4
	Mediterranean	674	12,729	355	0.122	0.007	14.1	1.3
Germany	Baden-Württemberg	735	13,837	282	0.148	0.016	14.0	1.4
	Bavaria	747	14,871	280	0.139	0.012	12.4	1.4
	Berlin	241	14,128	552	0.141	0.016	18.6	2.9
	Brandenburg/Mecklenburg-West Pomerania	449	12,613	255	0.105	0.012	15.0	1.9
	Hesse	395	15,024	423	0.154	0.014	15.4	2.0
	Lower Saxony/Bremen	526	13,852	270	0.162	0.024	13.8	1.7
	North Rhine-Westphalia	1,140	13,886	215	0.171	0.017	12.7	1.1
	Rhineland-Palatinate/Saarland	329	13,133	385	0.108	0.012	11.0	1.8
	Saxony	486	12,446	243	0.087	0.012	11.9	1.6
	Saxony-Anhalt	297	12,922	299	0.082	0.009	15.9	2.2
	Schleswig Holstein/Hamburg	195	14,019	530	0.111	0.020	8.8	2.2
	Thuringia	307	12,275	222	0.066	0.007	16.6	2.5
Austria	East	1,224	14,257	259	0.187	0.012	15.9	1.1
	South/West	1,591	13,304	219	0.139	0.010	15.0	0.9
Portugal	North/Central/Lisbon	1,864	7,119	116	0.235	0.012	23.7	0.9
	South/Islands	2,819	7,434	110	0.271	0.010	22.0	0.7
Spain	North West	750	8,965	220	0.191	0.015	17.7	1.4
	North East	801	11,294	238	0.161	0.013	9.7	1.0
	Madrid	507	13,017	364	0.241	0.027	10.2	1.3
	Central	894	7,352	160	0.212	0.018	27.6	1.5
	East	1,154	10,297	228	0.172	0.010	11.8	0.9
	South/Canaries	1,312	7,706	139	0.204	0.015	27.8	1.2

continued

Table D.2: contd.../

Country	Region	Sample size	Median income (PPS)		Inequality index (mean log dev)		Poverty rate (national benchmark)	
			Median	Standard error	Index	Standard error	%	Standard error
Italy	North West	602	12,299	366	0.143	0.011	9.9	1.3
	Lombardy	673	13,278	311	0.125	0.010	8.5	1.2
	North East	743	12,607	321	0.132	0.011	8.4	1.0
	Emilia-Romagna	359	13,195	451	0.137	0.026	8.2	1.7
	Central	704	11,859	343	0.132	0.012	10.3	1.3
	Lazio	418	10,450	373	0.165	0.019	17.8	2.0
	Abruzzo-Molise/Campania	998	8,693	176	0.158	0.010	28.2	1.4
	South	912	8,093	171	0.200	0.015	34.1	1.6
	Islands	961	7,960	147	0.221	0.013	36.6	1.6
Greece	Mainland	2,465	6,568	95	0.235	0.008	28.6	0.9
	Attica/Islands	1,521	9,218	193			13.2	0.8

See Appendix C for definitions of grouped regions.
All calculations based on weighted data, using the Stata analysis program.
The median and its standard error calculated using *quantile regression*.
The inequality index (mean logarithmic deviation) and its standard error calculated using *svygei3*, written by Stephen P. Jenkins.
The poverty rate and its standard error calculated using *svymean*.

Figure D.a: 95% confidence intervals around country median incomes

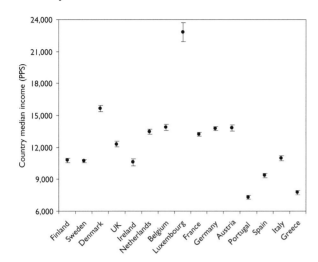

Figure D.b: 95% confidence intervals about regional median incomes in one example country: France

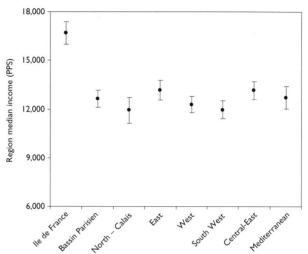

Table D.3: Regression equations showing the relationship between country and regional median incomes and various poverty rates

Definition of poverty line	60% of regional median	30% of regional 90th percentile	60% of country median	60% of European median
Country median income (000s)	−0.011	−0.026	−0.012	−0.059
(t ratio)	(6.1)	(8.8)	(5.5)	(20.3)
Regional median income (000s), as difference from country median	0.000	−0.005	−0.040	−0.048
(t ratio)	(0.0)	(0.9)	(9.6)	(8.5)
Constant	0.292	0.446	0.303	0.899
(t ratio)	(13.5)	(13.0)	(12.1)	(26.5
Adjusted R² (%)	39	58	68	89

Note: regression equation based on summary measures for region-groups – 61 observations. Sampling errors in the estimates of median incomes and poverty rates are not taken into account. t-ratios of less than 2 indicate an insignificant relationship.